The
Last Word

The
Last Word

A Sparkling Collection of Put-downs,
Epitaphs, Final Utterances, Touching Tributes
and Damning Dismissals

Donald Sinden

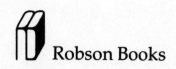

Robson Books

First published in Great Britain in 1994 by Robson Books Ltd,
Bolsover House, 5-6 Clipstone Street, London W1P 7EB

British Library Cataloguing in Publication Data
A catalogue record for this title is available from the British Library

ISBN 0 86051 892 2

Designed by Harold King

Typeset in Meridien by Columns Design and Production Services Ltd
Reading
Printed by Butler & Tanner Ltd., Frome and London

CONTENTS

INTRODUCTION

There is no denying that an actor always relishes having the last word – in any context. To have the last word leaves your audience, in its broadest sense, focused on you. It leaves them with your parting line echoing in their ears.

To put it simply, if you have the last you are remembered. This is what I hope to show in this collection of 'last words' which ranges from stylish put downs to wonderfully spontaneous *bon mots*, gathered far and wide – from the cut and thrust of the political stage to the dressing-rooms of the West End, from the intimacy of the boudoir to the eternal rest of the graveyard.

Quite often success with last words depends on providing your own cue lines, though there are those past masters like Oscar Wilde and Noël Coward who were able to conjure perfect last words from next to nothing. Emlyn Williams was the same. I have always enjoyed the story of the time he overheard a conversation between two women at a party in the course of which one remarked to the other, 'I hear that Noël's had a new set of false teeth made.'

'I wonder what he's going to do with the old set?' asked her companion.

At that moment Emlyn interjected, 'Have them made into a brooch for Joyce Carey.' How the rest of us yearn for that felicity with words; quickly and brilliantly crafted.

Similarly, at another cocktail party, two men are talking and one of them comments, 'I say, that girl on the other side of the room – she's the most amazingly beautiful thing I've seen for years. My golly she's attractive . . . Whatever happened to that silly little man she married?'

'I'm married to her,' replied his companion.

'Well, there you are. What happened to you?' retorted the first man, proving, if ever proof were needed, that attack is always the best means of defence.

The enduring quality of the last word is most frequently seen in the final utterances of those passing from this world to the next. Edmund Gwenn, the lovely, cuddly old character actor, known as Teddy, who made a great success in Hollywood was on his deathbed, watched over by a life-long friend. The old actor's breathing was laboured, leading his friend to ask, 'Is it difficult, Teddy?'

'Not nearly as difficult as playing comedy,' Teddy replied and died.

What would any actor give to go out on a line like that?

Stanley Holloway had other thoughts on his mind as he prepared to meet his maker. After his marathon run as Dolittle in *My Fair Lady* in New York and London, his part was taken over by James Hayter, who was famous for doing the voice-over for the advertisement for Mr Kipling's Cakes. Twenty years later, Stanley Holloway was slipping away and his son, Julian, was sitting by his bed recalling his career, 'Dad, you've had an amazing life. You've topped the bill in everything you've ever done: theatre, films, television, radio, the music hall, recordings. In everything you've ever touched you've topped the bill.'

'Not a bad life, not a bad life,' acknowledged his father.

'Do you have any regrets?' Julian asked.

'Yes . . . oh, yes,' said Stanley.

'Really . . . what are they?'

'I should have got that Mr Kipling voice-over,' said the great comedian as he closed his eyes for ever.

Here the irony which colours so many last words comes to the fore, perhaps expressed most tellingly in Hamlet's lines from the graveyard scene:

Imperious Caesar, dead and turn'd to clay,
Might stop a hole to keep the wind away:
0, that earth which kept the world in awe
Should patch a wall t'expel the winter's flaw.

That truly is a masterly 'last word' in every sense. Not all that follow are as profound, but I hope that you find them enjoyable and that some may leave an echo to provoke a chuckle long after you have finished the book.

1

JUST
BETWEEN
OURSELVES

'A husband,' wrote Helen Rowland, 'is what is left of a lover after the nerve has been extracted.' Neat (and possibly true) as the definition is, it cannot claim to be a universal maxim since many lovers never make it to the altar and others lose their nerve long before the prospect of a more lasting relationship ever arises.

The late Lady Veronica McLeod knew how to cool ardour as easily as she could arouse it – and she did both with consummate ease and style. The only daughter of a general stationed in India and a renowned beauty in the London of the 1890s she sailed to Bombay at the age of nineteen to spend a few months with her parents. In the course of the voyage she won the heart of a dashing steward looking after the needs of passengers travelling second class. At the ship's fancy dress ball they danced together before slipping away to her ladyship's cabin where they concluded a delightful evening together.

The steward was up and serving breakfast to his charges long before Lady Veronica awoke and when he tracked her down later in the day she reproved him icily for his familiarity. 'In the circles in which I move,' she explained, 'sleeping with a woman does not constitute an introduction.'

In selecting lovers, the byword must be caution. Maurice Chevalier observed, 'Many a man has fallen in

---

love with a girl in a light so dim he would not have chosen a suit by it.'

Elinor Glynn had these words of advice on would-be lovers:

Americans – fatherly and uncouth

French – passionate and *petit maître*

Austrian – sentimental and feckless

Hungarian – passionate and exacting

Scandinavian – psychological and scientific

Russian – passionate and unstable

Spanish – jealous and matter of fact

Italian – romantic and fickle

English – casual and adorable

German – sentimental and vulgar

All the near East – passionate and untrustworthy

Then there are those so unlucky in love that they never have a chance of qualifying for any of Ms Glynn's carefully chosen adjectives. One such was the sad British Rail employee whose unrequited passion led him to attempt suicide – five times. In death, as in love, he failed miserably.

Retelling his story for the benefit of readers of the *Whitley Bay Guardian* he catalogued his misadventures, all brought about by failing to win the affections of a girl he'd run across at the station where he worked:

'At 7.30 I had a drink and walked into the sea,' he began, 'but it was so wet I turned back, went home and by 9.15 I had wired up my easy chair to the mains. However, each time I threw the switch the power fused. Following this, I broke my mirror and tried to cut my

wrists, yet somehow the slashes were not deep enough.
After that I tried to hang myself from the banisters;
unfortunately the knot was improperly tied. Finally I surrounded myself with cushions and set them on fire. This
method was much too hot, so I jumped out of the window and telephoned the Samaritans but they were
constantly engaged.'

You can't always count on a sympathetic hearing when
you write to the papers for advice on affairs of the heart.
The *Singapore Free Press* printed a letter on its 'Uncle Joe'
Problem Page which told an all too familiar tale:

'I am an Indian; aged nineteen,' explained the correspondent, 'and I'm in love with a fifteen-year-old
Eurasian schoolgirl. I fell in love with her when she was
thirteen: but I was forced to "break-off" with her recently. The reasons for this are 1. She does not seem to care
for me of late; 2. She has started to mix with a set of bad
girls; 3. She thinks she can boss everybody. Also I have a
suspicion that she thinks I love someone else. Have I
done right by breaking away from her? What shall I do?'

In reply 'Uncle Joe' had this to say, 'I am getting rather
"fed up" with people who keep on writing on both sides
of the paper, as you have done. The next time anybody
does this, I'm going to throw his letter into the waste-
paper basket and say nothing.'

A letter written to the agony aunt on *Woman's Day*
required more delicate handling, 'My boyfriend is very
good looking,' it began eagerly, 'and we get on well
except that he is a "square" and I love jazz and jiving. He
says I am a case of arrested development, but my meas-
urements are 36,22,36. What does he mean?'

Nor is it invariably true that all the world loves a lover.
Another letter addressed to *Empire News* informed readers, 'Our holiday at Blackpool last week was ruined by

canoodling couples . . . My husband and I were terribly embarrassed because we had our two daughters, fourteen and sixteen, with us. For our next holiday (in July) we are going to Bournemouth. You don't see this shameless behaviour in the South.'

Here I must offer a word of contradiction. When I joined the Webber-Douglas School of Dramatic Art, the war was just over, the school having been evacuated to Hampshire and male students were still in short supply (there were six of us, three of whom were non-starters, so to speak). The combination of these ingredients topped up with thirty-one beautiful girls resulted in days of ceaseless distraction and nights of, well, considerable activity. I shared a room with Bill Pyman whose training at the Webber-Douglas was put to unexpected use one morning when matron returned some shirts from the laundry. As she put them into the drawer a packet of contraceptives was revealed. 'What are these?' she asked.

'They're something Donald uses for his asthma,' replied my resourceful room mate so plausibly that the good lady, a widow of many years, left quite satisfied.

Such unworldliness can have its downside as was the case of a twenty-five-year-old labourer whose 'prospects' suffered following an accident with a bulldozer. He took his case to court, claiming damages for an impaired sex life. His counsel argued forcibly that for a man of his age the consequences bordered on the tragic. The judge was less convinced and enquired whether the plaintiff was married. Hearing that he wasn't, he commented, 'Well, I cannot see how it affects his sex life.'

Two centuries earlier James Boswell had to face an impediment to his love life, uncomfortably common in those days. His own account takes the form of a 'scene' he recorded with the actress Mrs Louisa Lewis:

Thursday 20 January

I then went to Louisa. With excellent address did I
carry on this interview, as the following scene, I trust,
will make appear.

LOUISA   My dear Sir! I hope you are well
            today.
BOSWELL   Excessively well: I thank you. I hope I
            find you so.
LOUISA   No, really, Sir. I am distressed with a
            thousand things. (Cunning jade, her
            circum-stances!) I really don't know
            what to do.
BOSWELL   Do you know that I have been
            unhappy since I saw you?
LOUISA   How so, Sir?
BOSWELL   Why, I am afraid that you don't love
            me so well, nor have not such regard
            for me as I thought you had.
LOUISA   Nay, dear Sir! (Seeming unconcerned.)
BOSWELL   Pray, Madam, have I no reason?
LOUISA   No, indeed, Sir, you have not.
BOSWELL   Have I no reason, Madam? Pray think.
LOUISA   Sir!
BOSWELL   Pray, Madam, in what state of health
            have you been in for some time?
LOUISA   Sir, you amaze me.
BOSWELL   I have but too strong, too plain reason
            to doubt your regard. I have for some
            days observed the symptoms of
            disease, but was unwilling to believe
            you so very ungenerous. But now,
            Madam, I am thoroughly convinced.
LOUISA   Sir, you have terrified me. I protest I
            know nothing of the matter.

7

BOSWELL Madam, I have had no connection
with any woman but you these two
months, I was with my surgeon this
morning, who declared I had got a
strong infection and that she from
whom I had it could not be ignorant
of it . . . You have used me very ill. I
did not deserve it. You know you said
where there was no confidence, there
was no breach of trust. But surely I
placed some confidence in you. I am
sorry that I was mistaken.

LOUISA Sir, I will confess to you that about
three years ago I was very bad. But for
these fifteen months I have been quite
well. I appeal to God Almighty that I
am speaking true; and for these six
months I have had to do with no man
but yourself.

BOSWELL But by G—d, Madam, I have been
with none but you, and here I am
very bad.

LOUISA Well, Sir, by the same solemn oath I
protest that I was ignorant of it.

BOSWELL Madam, I wish much to believe you.
But I own I cannot upon this occasion
believe a miracle . . .

As I was going, said she, 'I hope, Sir, you will give me
leave to enquire after your health.' 'Madam,' said I,
archly, 'I fancy it will be needless for some weeks.' She
again renewed her request. But unwilling to be
plagued any more with her, I put her off by saying I
might perhaps go to the country, and left her.

Thus ended my intrigue with the fair Louisa, which

I flattered myself so much with, and from which I expected at least a winter's safe copulation.

(Mrs Louisa Lewis, typified the reputation sometimes unjustly attributed to many on the stage for possessing an active libido. I recall the story of the young actor who was seeking advice from an experienced colleague on the interpretation of the part of Hamlet. Was it not likely that Hamlet had been to bed with Ophelia, he wanted to know? 'I don't know about the West End, laddie,' advised the older actor, 'but we always did on tour.')

A contemporary of Louisa Lewis's, whose private life was equally colourful and adventurous, announced her intention to marry which aroused considerable comment. The actor and playwright Samuel Foote was with a group of friends when the subject of the forthcoming nuptials arose. 'It is a very good match she has made,' one of them commented.

'And they say she made to her husband a full confession of all her past affairs,' remarked one of the others.

'What honesty she must have had,' said a third.

'What courage!' – a fourth.

'What a memory!' added Foote.

The strategy for turning down an unwelcome proposal varies with the times. In 1834 it could be tackled like this:

After the decided disapprobation I have constantly evinced to your attentions, I was rather surprised at receiving an offer of marriage from you.

I am sorry that you have thus placed me under the disagreeable necessity of speaking on a subject so repugnant to my feelings; but candour and truth compel me to return an instant and positive negative to your proposal.

I trust, therefore, you will no longer persist in disturbing, by such unavailing efforts, the peace of sir, your obedient servant . . .

To transplant a phrase from this chilling retort to a steamier situation, John Aubrey recorded Sir Walter Raleigh's success when a 'positive negative' was far from the last word on the subject. 'He loved a wench well;' wrote Aubrey,' and one time getting one of the Maids of Honour up against a tree in a wood ('twas his first Lady) who seemed at first boarding to be somewhat fearful of her honour and modest, she cried: "Sweet Sir Walter, what do you ask me? Will you undo me? Nay, sweet Sir Walter! Sweet Sir Walter! Sir Walter!" At last, as the danger and the pleasure at the same time grew higher, she cried in the extasy, "Swisser Swatter, Swisser Swatter". She proved with child, and I doubt not but that this hero took care of them both, as also that the product was more than an ordinary mortal.'

A generation earlier Sir Thomas Wyatt contemplated the age of forty and concluded that the time had come at last to leave love to younger hearts:

Farewell, Love, and all thy laws forever.
Thy baited hooks shall tangle me no more;
Senec and Plato call me from thy lore,
To perfect wealth my wit for to endeavour.
In blind error when I did persevere,
Thy sharp repulse, that pricketh aye so sore,
Hath taught me to set in trifles no store
And scape forth since liberty is lever.
Therefore farewell. Go trouble younger hearts

And in me claim no more authority.
With idle youth go use thy property
And thereon spend thy many brittle darts:
For hitherto though I have lost all my time,
Me lusteth no longer rotten boughs to climb.

(The American writer and humorist, Robert Benchley, was less inclined to make way for a younger generation. At the start of a Hollywood party Benchley drew considerable satisfaction as the outstanding ladies' man present. Then, as a couple of younger matinée idols arrived, girls started to drift away and one unwisely commented to Benchley before swapping allegiances, 'Now, that's my idea of real he-men.'

Benchley was not impressed. 'He-men', he scoffed, 'I'll bet the hair of their combined chests wouldn't make a wig for a grape.')

The poet Robert Herrick, shared Sir Thomas Wyatt's advice in what is probably his best known poem. If lusty swains needed any encouragement, this is surely the 'last word' on courtship:

Gather ye rose-buds while ye may,
Old Time is still a-flying:
And this same flower that smiles today,
Tomorrow will be dying.

The glorious lamp of heaven, the sun
The higher he's a-getting,
The sooner will his race be run,
And nearer he's to setting.

The age is best which is the first,
When youth and blood are warmer;
But being spent, the worse, and worst
Times still succeed the former.

Then be not coy, but use your time;
And while ye may, go marry:
For having lost but once your prime,
You may for ever tarry.

(Herrick would be comforted to find his advice taken centuries later. General M W Clarke, who was in charge of the American ground forces in Europe during the First World War, was once asked what was the best advice he had ever been given. He answered. 'To marry the girl I did.'

'And who gave you that advice?'

'She did,' replied the general.)

John Donne, Herrick's senior by some twenty years, followed his natural urges too enthusiastically for his own good, when at around Christmas 1600 he secretly married Anne More. She was the niece of his employer, Sir Thomas Egerton, and the discovery of their marriage led to Donne's dismissal and imprisonment.

Although the couple were subsequently forgiven and allowed to enjoy sixteen years of happy married life, they were forced to part when their secret was revealed. At the bottom of a letter to his wife, the poet wrote a telling final sentence, 'John Donne, Anne Donne, Un-done.'

Unhappily what love there had been in the marriage of the later seventeenth century poet, John Dryden, soon turned to loathing. Dryden's marriage was notoriously miserable. His wife Elizabeth once complained that he spent far more time in his library than with her, 'Lord Mr Dryden! How can you always be poring over those musty books. I wish I were a book, and then I should have more of your company.'

'Pray, my dear,' he replied, 'if you do become a book let it be an almanac, for then I shall change you every year.'

The 'mad, bad and dangerous to know' Lord Byron was already tiring of his relationship with Lady Caroline Lamb when she broke into his rooms and, across the title page of one of his books, wrote, 'Remember me.' He responded with this short verse:

Remember thee! Remember thee!
Till Lethe quench life's burning streams
Remorse and shame shall cling to thee
And haunt thee like a feverish dream
Remember thee! Ay, doubt it not,
Thy husband too shall think of thee,
By neither shalt thou be forgot,
Thou false to him, thou fiend to me!

Helen Rowland, as we have already discovered, viewed marriage through anything but rose-tinted glasses. 'When you see what some girls marry,' she noted, 'you realize how they must hate to work for a living.' More depressingly she also commented, 'When a girl marries she exchanges the attentions of many men for the inattention of one.'

Views of marriage are blurred from an early age if the views of the following two young girls are any guide. The first was a candidate for confirmation in a small rural community. One day her confirmation class was visited by the archbishop and to her dismay the priest asked her to define the state of matrimony. 'It's a state of terrible torment which those who enter are compelled to undergo for a time to prepare them for a better world,' she answered.

'No, no,' snapped the priest, 'that's not matrimony. That's the definition of Purgatory.'

'Leave her alone,' said the archbishop, 'perhaps the child has been shown the light.'

The other little girl, somewhat younger, amused the writer George Ade, who enjoyed recounting their meeting: 'I was sitting with a little girl of eight one afternoon. She looked up from the copy of Hans Andersen she was reading, and asked innocently, "Does m-i-r-a-g-e spell marriage, Mr Ade?" "Yes, my child," said I.'

Can I slip in a story told to me by Dean Peck, Dean of Lincoln, which has always amused me. This concerned the Bishop of Lincoln, one of whose pastoral duties in the early 1960s was to visit schools in the diocese. For him the opening gambit, rather than the last word, was always tricky until he hit upon a winning formula. He devised three questions that never failed to catch the children's attention. First he would ask a class, 'Now children, what is a mitre?' Quite often they would know that it is the hat the bishop wears. Question number two was a little harder, 'What is a crozier?' Perhaps only a few would be able to identify it as the shepherd's crook the bishop carries. The last question was the killer, 'What is a pectoral cross?' Never in his experience had any child known that this is the cross the bishop wears and in his experience this never failed to fire their interest. At one school, however, a teacher was present during this interrogation whose class the bishop was due to visit shortly. She slipped back to her charges and primed them with the right answers before the bishop's arrival. So when the bishop opened his talk in her class, 'Now children, can anyone tell me what is a mitre,' they answered to a child, 'It's the hat the bishop wears.'

'Yes . . . ' he answered, 'and what is a crozier?'

'It's the shepherd's crook that the bishop carries,' chimed the children in unison.

Suspecting some underhand work, he offered his third question, 'Right children, what is an archdeacon?'

A moment's silence followed, until it was broken by a small voice exclaiming enthusiastically, 'It's the cross that the bishop carries round his neck.'

Lilian Baylis had a notorious reputation for discouraging romances within her companies. The story is told of a young actor and actress who presented themselves in front of her desk, hand in hand. For a time she appeared not to notice them, then, barely raising her eyes from her desk she asked, 'Well, what is it?'

'We're in love, Miss Baylis,' the actor began, abashed, 'and we . . . er . . . we want to get married.'

'Go away,' she told them. 'I haven't got time to listen to gossip.'

During his time as Chancellor of West Germany Konrad Adenauer received many proposals of marriage through the post. They continued to arrive when he was well into his eighties but his request to his secretary was always the same, 'Put them into the non-aggression pact file.'

Some proposals fail for quite unexpected reasons. Lytton Strachey revealed an interesting sidelight on the marriage of Leonard and Virginia Woolf in a letter to Lady Ottoline Morrell: 'There's a story that a week or two before the engagement he proposed in a train, and she accepted him, but owing to the rattling of the carriage he didn't hear, and took up the newspaper again, saying "What?" On which she had a violent revulsion and replied, "Oh, nothing!"'

According to Erica Jong, 'Bigamy is having one husband too many. Monogamy is the same.' There may well have been times when Barbara Hutton, heiress to the Woolworth fortune, had wished Ms Jong's pronouncement had been made in time to spare her even a few of her seven marriages.

Miss Hutton first tied the knot in June 1933. The setting was Paris, the church a Russian cathedral and her husband a little known Georgian aristocrat who styled himself Prince Alexis Mdivani. In spite of an allowance of $50,000 a year, which his wife thoughtfully provided for him, Prince Mdivani showed signs of restlessness as early as the first night of their honeymoon. As Miss Hutton's lavishly equipped train sped towards her Italian villa, she squeezed her ample form into a silk nightdress, selected from one of the thirteen suitcases that constituted her trousseau. Watching in silence, her husband's eyes were fixed on her, and remained so as he told her, 'Barbara, you are too fat.'

The marriage lasted until May 1935 when the couple parted. Said Miss Hutton, 'I shall never marry again.' However, twenty-four hours after the divorce was finalized she married husband number two, Count Kurt Heinrich Haughwitz-Hardenberg-Reventlow. The breakup of that marriage cost Miss Hutton $375,000 and caused a momentary pause in her flirtation with minor European royalty.

Husband number three was Cary Grant. Hollywood called it the 'Cash and Cary marriage' but it lasted a bare three years and not for the first time Barbara Hutton left the divorce court vowing, 'I will never marry again. You cannot go on being fooled for ever.'

But she could and she did. Cary Grant was followed in 1947 by Prince Igor Troubetzkoy, a Lithuanian exile of, some claimed, dubious origin. Whatever his background, as a husband he was left wanting and Miss Hutton was soon calling him 'the meanest man in the world'. For his part the prince left the scene with $1,000 a month, for life.

As a 'golden hello' Barbara Hutton's fifth husband, the

Dominican diplomat-cum-playboy Porfirio Rubirosa, was given a string of polo ponies and his own aeroplane. On the day of the wedding several New York papers displayed a picture of the groom's ex-girlfriend, Zsa Zsa Gabor, sporting the black eye she claimed Rubirosa had given her when she refused to marry him. Wishing the couple 'all happiness', she added charitably, 'I'm so glad he got married, or I probably would never have been able to get rid of him.' (This didn't exactly square with her other celebrated remark that Rubirosa was 'to lovemaking what Tiffany is to diamonds'.) She gave the marriage six months – and over-estimated by more than three. 'Don't call me Mrs Rubirosa,' Miss Hutton chided.

She had another crack at royalty with her sixth husband, the German tennis star Baron Gottfried von Cramm. He got a set of pearl studs as a wedding present and his wife's assurances, 'I should have married him eighteen years ago.' His enthusiasm matched hers, 'I've been trying to marry her since I met her.' But within three years familiar rumours started circulating that marriage number six was heading the same way as all the others. The couple vehemently disagreed. He told the press the story was, 'Ridiculous! Only business commitments have kept us apart. Ours is a perfect marriage.' She agreed, 'I swear I have never been so happy and contented before.' However, a year later, following a discreet divorce, she confided, 'I'm as free as the air – no strings. I'm in no hurry to go through all that crazy routine again.'

To an extent this was true because it took her three years before plucking up the courage for marriage number seven. 'It's my lucky number,' she assured the world. 'This is my seventh husband. We were married at seven pm on 7 April. I have never been so happy in my life.'

The lucky man was another prince, from south-east Asia this time, one Raymond Doan Vinh Champacak. Disposing of him just over two years later cost her a further $3 million, according to unofficial reports. In some respects it was money well spent as, lucky or not, Barbara Hutton's seventh marriage was also her last.

Perhaps she would have been well advised to pay greater attention to the warnings Zsa Zsa Gabor regularly dished out, in spite of clocking up seven marriages herself. Appearing on television in a panel of experts who were being consulted on marital problems, she was asked by a young lady, 'I'm breaking my engagement to a very wealthy man who has already given me a sable coat, diamonds, a stove and a Rolls-Royce. What should I do?'

'Give back the stove,' Zsa Zsa told her.

On another television show called *Bachelor's Haven* a viewer had written in with this problem, 'My husband is a travelling salesman, but I know he strays when he is at home. How can I stop him?'

'Shoot him in the legs,' was the actress's simple solution.

Though she also cautioned, 'Husbands are like fires; they go out if they're unattended.'

There may be something in the Hungarian psyche that leads to this pragmatism. The novelist Ferenc Molnar shared it. He was philosophical after returning to Budapest from a tour abroad to have his mistress's infidelities detailed by friends. 'That's all right,' he assured them. 'She goes to bed with others because she loves them. But for money – only with me.'

The American writer and actress, Ilka Chase, had been married to Louis Calhern, who divorced her in order to marry Julia Hoyt. As she was sorting through her possessions not long after the unhappy episode she found some visiting cards that she had printed for herself with the name Mrs Louis Calhern. Generously, and mindful of her own experience, she posted them to her successor with the note, 'Dear Julia, I hope these reach you in time.'

Charmian Brent, the estranged wife of the Great Train Robber, Ronnie Biggs, was less magnanimous. Having escaped to Brazil, her husband claimed protected status under that country's law on the grounds that his girl-friend, Ramona, was pregnant with their child. Back at home Mrs Biggs remarked, 'For a pregnant Brazilian girl Ron's a prime catch.'

Queen Alexandra, the tolerant and impressively under-standing wife of Edward VII, demonstrated one of her best qualities when she commented wryly on his death, 'Now at least I know where he is!'

If Edward VII had failed as a model husband, he had a great deal to live up to in his father. Four years before Albert's death, Queen Victoria had written to her eldest son, 'None of you can ever be proud enough of being the child of such a Father who has not his equal in this world – so great, so good, so faultless. Try, all of you to follow in his footsteps and don't be discouraged, for to be really in everything like him none of you, I am sure, will ever be. Try, therefore, to be like him in some points, and you will have acquired a great deal.'

Once a widow, Queen's Victoria's standards of virtuous behaviour were even more impossible. When Disraeli's wife once suggested that her eldest son must be a great comfort to the queen, Victoria retorted, 'Comfort! Why, I caught him smoking a fortnight after his dear father died!'

Albert wasn't without a trace of humour, however. There's an engaging story told of him at Balmoral, where he was showing family pictures to a party of guests. One picture displayed all the royal children accompanied by an assortment of birds and animals. Someone asked which of the girls was Princess Helena. 'There, with the kingfisher,' replied her father, 'a very proper bird for a princess.'

As Queen Caroline, wife of George II, lay on her death-bed she encouraged him to marry again. When he pleaded that he could not take another wife but would rather have mistresses she rallied enough to retort, 'That shouldn't hamper your marrying.'

That said, they were a devoted couple. Horace Walpole recorded, 'It is certain that the King always preferred the Queen's person to that of any other woman; nor ever described his idea of beauty, but he drew the picture of his wife. They always went to bed on his return from Hanover as soon as he came out of the drawing-room, as at all times they did after dinner.'

In more recent times the marriage of the Duke and Duchess of Windsor belied much of the antagonism gen-erated by the abdication issue. Loyal and loving to the end, the Duchess was also candid about their relation-ship. Remarking once on her husband's preference for a simple salad, eaten alone in the middle of the day, she said, 'I married the Duke for better or worse, but not for lunch.'

The correspondent who wrote this letter to a woman's magazine reflected commendable steadfastness, 'I fell in love with my husband simply because he was so different from every other boy I had ever met. He did not like love-making, neither did I. Now after twenty-six years of marriage I sometimes wonder if I have missed something, but I am happy. He's a wonderful husband. He never actually proposed, but we saw a three-piece suite we both liked and that clinched the deal.'

Less felicitous was the state of the woman who

explained to a court in London, 'My husband is a jolly good sort, one of those very hearty men. He wears plus-fours, smokes a pipe, and talks about nothing but beer and rugby football. My nerves won't stand much more of it.'

For women faced with nagging anxieties about their marriages the magazine *Housewife* had this advice, 'If you want to know whether you are physically in love with your husband, I suggest in all seriousness that you should ask yourself the test question, "Could I use his tooth-brush?"'

I remember Maurice, a workmate from my days as an apprentice joiner, offering the same down-to-earth assessment.

'How long have you been married, Tom?' he asked a lorry driver.

'Three years,' was the answer.

'Just started farting in front of yer missus then.'

When a friend of Dr Johnson's lost his wife, after a notoriously unhappy marriage and promptly took a second bride, Johnson observed that this was a good example of 'the triumph of hope over experience'.

Dorothy Parker went one better and married her husband, Alan Campbell, twice. When they were married the second time she remarked at the reception, 'People who haven't talked to each other for years are on speaking terms – including the bride and groom.'

When Alan Campbell died, the playwright Lillian Hellman recorded a telling incident as Dorothy Parker watched his body being carried from the house, 'Among the friends who stood with Dottie on those California steps was Mrs Jones, a woman who had liked Alan, pretended to like Dottie, and who always loved all forms of meddling in other people's troubles. Mrs Jones said, "Dottie, tell me, dear what can I do for you."

'Dottie said, "Get me a new husband."

'There was a silence, but before those who would have laughed could laugh, Mrs Jones said, "I think that is the most callous and disgusting remark I ever heard in my life."

'Dottie turned to look at her, sighed, and said gently, "So sorry. Then run down to the corner and get a ham and cheese on rye and tell them to hold the mayo."'

Last-minute weakness left a German wife with the husband she had been trying to ditch, as became clear in a Dortmund court where she was seeking a divorce. The day before the hearing she had been to her husband's office to clear up a few minor details about the disposal of their property. Her husband used this opportunity to try to persuade her to change her mind, but the court heard that he had tried in vain. So it took everyone by surprise, the wife included, when her husband shouted, 'It's a lie', on hearing her tell the judge that they had last made love 'at least eighteen months ago'.

'We made love on the floor of my office yesterday morning!' the husband insisted, concluding triumphantly, 'I can prove it. I marked her bottom with the office date stamp.'

In *Oliver Twist* Dickens captured the charmless state of the Bumble marriage in this scene:

> 'I sold myself,' said Mr Bumble . . . 'for six teaspoons, a pair of sugar-tongs, and a milk-pot; with a small quantity of second-hand furniture and twenty pounds in money. I went very reasonable. Cheap, dirt cheap!'
>
> 'Cheap!' cried a shrill voice in Mr Bumble's ear: 'you would have been dear at any price; and dear enough I paid for you, Lord above knows that! . . . '

'Mrs Bumble, ma'am!' said Mr Bumble with senti-mental sternness . . .

'Are you going to sit there, all day?' inquired Mrs Bumble.

'I am going to sit here, as long as I think proper, ma'am,' rejoined Mr Bumble; 'and although I was not snoring, I shall snore, gape, sneeze, laugh, or cry, as the humour strikes me; such being my prerogative.'

'Your prerogative!' sneered Mrs Bumble, with inef-fable contempt.

'I said the word ma'am,' said Mr Bumble. 'The pre-rogative of man is to command.'

'And what is the prerogative of woman, in the name of Goodness?' cried the relict of Mr Corney deceased.

'To obey, ma'am,' thundered Mr Bumble. 'Your late unfortunate husband should have taught it to you; and then, perhaps, he might have been alive now. I wish he was, poor man!'

The following lines might have given Mr Bumble cause for reflection:

Last night I slew my wife,
Stretched her on the parquet flooring;
I was loth to take her life,
But I had to stop her snoring.

Alternatively he might have taken independent advice before popping the question. A young lady who sent a sample of her boyfriend's handwriting to a graphologist had a nasty shock. She had noticed an advertisement in the local press offering to tell fortunes for a modest fee and answered it with a covering note, 'Please find enclosed an example of my boyfriend's writing. Can you tell me if he would make a good husband?'

The return post brought the graphologist's answer, 'No, I'm afraid he won't, my dear. He's been a pretty rotten one to me for the last three years. But thanks for the evidence.'

Chico Marx was more accomplished in carrying off his infidelities. When his wife caught him kissing a chorus girl he explained, 'I wasn't kissing her. I was whispering in her mouth.'

Groucho would have concurred. 'They say a man is as old as the woman he feels,' he wrote in *The Secret World Is Groucho*. 'In that case I'm eighty-five . . . I want it known here and now that this is what I want on my tombstone. Here lies Groucho Marx, and Lies and Lies and Lies. P.S. He never kissed an ugly girl.'

Writing to a friend when he had reached his sixties, Groucho confessed, 'My sex life is now reduced to fan letters from an elderly lesbian who would like to borrow $800; phone calls from a flagrant fairy with chronic low blood pressure (he'd like to get into pictures); and Pincus's dog who howls mournfully under my window every night.'

Oscar Wilde renounced relationships with the opposite sex for well publicized reasons. It was W B Yeats who described what happened when he was persuaded to refresh his acquaintance in a French brothel following his release from prison:

Wilde had arrived in Dieppe, and Dowson pressed upon him the necessity of acquiring 'a more wholesome taste'. They emptied their pockets onto the café table, and though there was not much, there was enough, if both heaps were put into one. Meanwhile the news had spread, and they set out accompanied by a cheering crowd. Arrived at their destination, Dowson and the crowd remained outside, and presently Wilde returned. He said in a low voice to Dowson, 'The first these ten years, and it will be the last. It was like cold mutton' . . . and then aloud, so that the crowd might hear him, 'But tell it in England, for it will entirely restore my character.'

Let me side-step for a moment with a couple of stories, told to me by the critic James Agate, which I have always enjoyed. Agate was a homosexual cast in the 'bull queen' mode. Short, bulky, with a large bony head, he could have been boxing promoter.

The first tale concerns a journey he undertook by chauffeur-driven car up the Great North Road for an appointment somewhere in the Midlands. Pressed for time, after a late start, Agate urged his driver to keep up his speed as they passed through a sleepy village, the tranquillity of which should have been assured by the thirty mph signs standing at either end. Sure enough a police motor cyclist, lying in wait out of sight, overtook the speeding limousine and flagged it down. The officer took his time dismounting, removing his gauntlets and walking up to the car. As he bent down to speak to the driver his demeanour changed markedly. 'Hello!' he said, and putting his head inside gave the driver a smacking kiss full on the lips before adding, 'Get going and don't get caught again.'

'Do you know him?' asked the astonished Agate, as they drove on.

'I can't remember his name, sir,' replied the chauffeur, 'but we were in the Guards together.'

The other story I like centres on Agate's surprising interest in keeping a string of trotting ponies. One day he

invited the president of the national trotting pony associ-
ation to lunch at his flat. This may not have been a wise
choice as the president was a brigadier of the old school
and almost all the block's residents, including the staff,
were homosexual.

After lunch, served by his 'manservant', host and guest
decided to go for a walk, but as they stepped out of the
lift on the ground floor Agate realized that he'd left his
walking stick behind. Addressing the hall porter in sten-
torian tones, he said, 'Get through to my man and tell
him to bring my stick.'

This he did by means of the house telephone, picking
up the receiver, pressing Agate's number and, overheard
by the brigadier, saying, 'Is that you Emma? She's forgotten her wand again.'

Oscar Wilde's disillusionment with women in bed
reflected a fundamental lack of interest. In the case of
Algernon Swinburne it boiled down to a lack of practice.
He only managed one fully fledged affair with a mature
woman and that wasn't a rip-roaring success. At its
height his middle-aged paramour was heard to complain,
'I can't seem to make him understand that biting's no
good.'

Others who suffer from sexual inadequacy choose to
manifest it in a different way. I admire the drama student
(female) who came out of a public telephone box one
evening to be confronted with one of the raincoat brigade
exposing himself. 'What do you think of that, then?' he
urged.

'It looks like a prick to me,' she said pushing her way
past him, 'only smaller.'

Several years ago the *Daily Mail* discussed how a flasher
might be dealt with on a golf course. 'I read with interest,' explained the correspondent, 'of the lady golfer who,

when confronted by a naked man wearing only a bowler hat, asked him whether he was a member, and then hit him with a Number 8 iron.

'Purists will long dispute whether it was obviously a mashie-shot, or whether the niblick should have been used. I hold no strong views myself. But I do wonder what the lady would have done had the man produced from his bowler hat a valid membership card.'

This reminds me of the superbly tongue-in-cheek review of *Lady Chatterley's Lover* which appeared in the American sporting magazine *Field and Stream*:

This pictorial account of the day-to-day life of an English gamekeeper is full of considerable interest to outdoor minded readers, as it contains many passages on pheasant-raising, the apprehending of poachers, ways to control vermin, and other chores and duties of the professional gamekeeper. Unfortunately, one is obliged to wade through many pages of extraneous material in order to discover and savour those side-lights on the management of a midland shooting estate, and in this reviewer's opinion the book cannot take the place of J R Miller's *Practical Gamekeeping*.

The relationship portrayed in D H Lawrence's novel no doubt had its moments, but it hardly stands as a formula for wedded bliss. For that Lawrence's contemporaries drew some inspiration from the unlikely source of Beatrice and Sidney Webb, the early socialists and social reformers. Bertrand Russell had this to say about them, 'Sidney and Beatrice Webb . . . were the most completely married couple I have ever known. They were, however, very averse from any romantic view of love or marriage. Marriage was a social institution designed to fit instinct into a legal framework. During the first ten years of their marriage, Mrs Webb would remark at intervals, "as Sidney always says, marriage is the waste-paper basket of the emotions."'

Bernard Shaw was more red-blooded 'How did the idea enter into your head that their relationship was frigid and inhuman? I used to live with them, and work with them a good deal, and you may take it from me that you couldn't be more wrong. Though Sidney, when they were working together, could stick it out almost indefinitely, Beatrice would suddenly reach the end of her tether, jump up, throw her pen away, fling herself on her husband, and half smother him with kisses. This might happen two or three times in a morning; and after each outbreak she would return to work with new vigour, and grind away like a slave until the need for a similar stimulant became imperative.'

I think the last word should be left to the lady herself, paying a tender and loving tribute to her husband. 'Sidney is simply unconscious of all the little meanness which turns social intercourse sour,' she wrote, 'he is sometimes tired, occasionally bored, but never unkindly or anxious to shine, or be admired, and wholly unaware of the absence of, or presence of, social consideration. I verily believe that if he were thrown . . . into a company of persons all of whom wanted to snub him, he would take up the first book and become absorbed in it, with a sort of feeling that they were good-natured enough not to claim his attention, or that they did not perceive that he was reading on the sly. And the greater personages they happened to be, the more fully satisfied he would be with the arrangement; since it would relieve him of any haunting fear that he was neglecting his social duty and making others uncomfortable. On the other hand,

whether in his own house or ain another's, if some person is neglected or out of it, Sidney will quite
unconsciously drift to them and be seen eagerly talking to
them.'

2

ABSURD
PERSON
SINGULAR

I have to confess that I am terrible at remembering names. Learning a part has seldom been a problem. But mention a name in passing and you can be sure it will pass straight by me.

During my time with the Rankery, as we came to call the Rank Organization, I must have opened hundreds of fêtes, shops, bazaars and sporting events and, as you can imagine, this problem with names led to some extremely uncomfortable moments.

On one occasion I was called upon to open a fête which was attended by the president of whichever organization was going to benefit from the proceeds and was also held in the grounds of his magnificent home. It would be prudent, to say the least, to mention him in my opening remarks. At our introduction, however, I had only grasped his rank, 'brigadier'. His name eluded me completely.

'Excuse me,' I enquired surreptitiously of two ladies sitting away from the main gathering, 'could you tell me the name of the brigadier.'

'Oh, yes – Brigadier Brkstdl,' which frankly left me none the wiser.

'I'm so sorry, I didn't quite . . . '

'Brigadier Brkstdl.'

'Would you mind spelling that?'

'B-R-E-A-K-S-T-E-D-D-L-E.'

' . . . and how do you pronounce it?'

'Brkstdl.'

'You must be joking!'

'No. He's my husband.'

(In this respect I could even feel a tinge of sympathy for Richard Nixon who was signing copies of his book *Six Crises* and, as he did, asking each customer to whom it should be inscribed. 'You've just met your seventh crisis,' one man told him with a grin. 'My name is Stanislaus Wojechzleschki.' I get most of my good stories from my next-door neighbour Edward Mautner, and one of my favourites concerns another Polish man who needed his eyes testing. He went to an optician and sat facing the familiar chart with letters of varying sizes and a bottom line which read something like C Z Y U P H V. 'Can you read that?' asked the optician. 'Read it?' asked the Polish man, 'I know him!')

I fared no better with names at a charity ball where I had the great good fortune to be taken in hand by a lady who knew everyone and everything about them in the nicest possible way. She guided me effortlessly from group to group, performed gracious introductions, massaged some amusing small talk and then gently moved me on to my next assignment. Beside her I was completely at ease. But as soon as she left, I was stranded.

'You don't remember where we last met,' said one of two men I found myself talking to alone, reading the look of bewilderment on my face with telling accuracy. 'Well, you stayed the weekend with us in Suffolk,' he continued.

'But of course!' I answered lamely. 'Yes, yes, I remember . . . '

Reunited with my Lady Bountiful I had to know, 'Quick, quick, who the hell is that man standing in the corner?'

Even she was slightly thrown by this as she said, 'My husband, of course.'

(Thankfully I am not alone among actors when it comes to difficulty with names. Walter Hudd, who directed me once at Stratford in *Dr Faustus*, found himself sitting through a play next to a man whose face was tantalizingly familiar but whose identity completely eluded him. Right through the first act he cast tentative glances at his neighbour trying to figure out who on earth he was. The play was a lost cause as he cudgelled his brain, in the interval going for a drink to search for inspiration. Standing at the bar he found the same man right by him. He had no choice but to ask outright, 'Forgive me, but don't I know you?'

'Yes,' said the stranger, 'I'm your agent.'

Ralph Richardson was the same. A story, surely apocryphal, but engaging all the same, tells of his approaching a man on a station platform and exclaiming, 'My dear Robertson! How you've changed! You look so much younger – your face is round – you've got a good colour – you've shaved off your moustache – my, how you've changed!'

'But my name isn't Robertson,' replied the other man.

'What! Changed your name too,' said Ralph.

In the days when he, Laurence Olivier and John Burrell were fellow directors of the Old Vic, they got together for a precious hour between rehearsals to discuss something of vital importance concerning the company's future policy. The chosen rendezvous was a pub in St Martin's Lane, at the entrance to which Ralph was waylaid by a man who asked him something. The others found a table where they sat fuming for twenty minutes before Ralph finally joined them full of apologies.

'Who the hell was that?' demanded Olivier.

'I don't know, Larry,' said Ralph. 'He thought he had seen us somewhere before, and I was trying to help him remember where.'

John Gregson, who joined the Rankery shortly before me, used to tell a similar story against himself, concerning *Genevieve,* one of his most successful films.

He was having a quiet drink in his local one evening when a voice behind him said, 'Old cars. London to Brighton. Need I say more?'

'Yes. You're quite right,' answered John with little enthusiasm.

His fellow drinker gave a thumbs-up sign to his chums seated at a table, mouthed 'Yes: it is!' and then said to John, 'What did you say your name is?'

'John Gregson,' was the modestly whispered reply.

'I'm sorry, I'm a bit hard of hearing. What did you say?'

'John Gregson,' said my friend, as distinctly and as close to the other fellow's ear as he could.

The answer was not what the other man was expecting. 'No, it's not him,' he mouthed to the group at the table. ''Ere – what was the name of the *funny* one in that film?'

'Do you mean Kenneth More?' John asked, mildly exasperated.

This did the trick. 'Yeah, yeah – Kenneth More – cor *he* was *funny'* and he went back to his friends repeating, 'Kenneth More. Yeah. Kenneth More.'

Another time John and I were in a restaurant together with our wives when a man came up and asked me, 'You're Terence Morgan aren't you?'

'No, he's not,' butted in John, 'but you're very lucky tonight because neither am I.'

This pleased the enquirer no end and he went off muttering, 'Thank you – thank you.'

Sir Thomas Beecham had trouble with names too. The Beecham story with which I have greatest empathy took place in Fortnum and Mason's. Beecham was in a throng gathered at a counter trying to pay for whatever he had purchased and having some difficulty in attracting the assistant's attention. In the midst of this a woman's voice behind him said, 'Good morning, Sir Thomas.'

'Good morning,' he replied with scarcely a glance in her direction.

'I'm delighted to see you,' continued the lady. 'We did enjoy your concert last week.'

'Thank you,' answered Beecham with the growing awareness that he was supposed to know her. 'You're keeping well?' he enquired.

'Yes, thank you.'

'How are the children?'

'They're very well, thank you.'

'And your husband . . . what's he up to these days?'

'He's still king you know.'

Sir Malcolm Sargent was not much better. When a member of a Scandinavian royal family attended one of his concerts, Sargent hurried round in the interval to introduce the leading soloist.

'Your Majesty, may I present Sergio Poliakoff?' he said proudly. 'Sergio – the King of Norway.'

The tall, distinguished figure shifted uncomfortably and murmured, 'Sweden, actually.'

During the First World War an American officer came across a fresh-faced English officer close to the front line and asked his identity.

'The Prince of Wales,' said the younger pleasantly as they passed.

'Is that right?' said the American with an air of strong disbelief. 'And I'm the King of England.'

A few nights later they were together again at a Red Cross station where the English officer's identity was confirmed to the American's acute embarrassment. Worse was to come. The prince spotted him in the crowd, waved and shouted across the hubbub, 'Hello there, dad.'

Towards the end of the Prince's father's reign the first Belisha beacons began to appear on British streets. George V was eager to put one of the new pedestrian crossings to the test. Driving in London soon after their introduction, he asked his chauffeur to pull over, so he could try one out. The trial run seemed satisfactory and a few minutes later the King Emperor got back into his limousine in great good spirits, declaring, 'One of my devoted subjects has just called me a doddering old idiot.'

One of his granddaughter's subjects got off less lightly when he greeted the Duke of Edinburgh at a regional airport and asked whether he had a good flight.

'Have you ever flown?' asked Prince Philip.

'Yes, sir, often.'

'Well, it was just like that.'

When Edith Sitwell was in America she was asked by a pushy reporter, 'Why do you call yourself "Dame"?'

'I don't,' replied the poetess. 'The Queen does.'

(With the same lofty dismissiveness Barbara Cartland established her own credentials when she was interviewed on the radio after the announcement of the engagement of the Prince and Princess of Wales. Asked whether she thought that class barriers had broken down in this country, she replied, 'Of course they have, or I wouldn't be sitting here talking to someone like you.')

As well as building Her Majesty's Theatre, Sir Herbert Beerbohm Tree, owned it, ran it, staged his own plays there and was the leading man. With quite a lot on his plate he always had a number of things on his mind in addition to his own performance. One day he was called from his dressing-room down to the stage dressed as Svengali, with a huge black beard and massive wig of mad dark hair. Waiting at the stage door was someone to see him, but Tree, preoccupied, passed him without stopping, only to come hurrying back. Profuse with apologies he explained, 'My dear fellow, I'm so sorry. I didn't recognize you in my beard.'

The mother of the American novelist and playwright, Carson McCullers, struck up a friendly conversation with a lady of aristocratic bearing on a train bound for New York. Having noticed that her companion was fond of reading, Mrs Cullers's mother explained that she was going to visit her 'writer' daughter and then embarked on a lengthy description of her unsurpassed literary talents. The other lady listened attentively for some time before mentioning that her father had also been a writer. Mrs McCullers's mother asked his name.

'Count Tolstoy,' was the answer.

It was unusual for strangers to get the better of Bernard Shaw but a country clergyman who wrote to him managed with some style. He had contacted Shaw for his recipe for brewing coffee, having heard that the playwright was considered to be an expert. Shaw obligingly sent it to him, though he couldn't resist a postscript stating that he hoped this wasn't a subtle ploy for getting his autograph. The clergyman wrote to thank Shaw for the recipe and included in the envelope Shaw's signature cut from his letter. 'I wrote in good faith,' read the letter of thanks, 'so allow me to return what it is obvious you infinitely prize, but which is of no value to me, your autograph.'

It wasn't unknown for Shaw to return 'at home' cards with the inscription 'GBS also' but Edmund Wilson, the American critic and essayist, went one better. In order to stem the constant flow of letters from complete strangers wanting advice or help on a whole range of subjects, he had a card printed which read, 'Edmund Wilson regrets that it is impossible for him to: Read manuscripts, write articles or books to order, write forewords or introductions, make statements for publicity purposes, do any kind of editorial work, judge literary contests, give interviews, take part in writers' conferences, answer questionnaires, contribute to or take part in symposiums or panels of any kind, contribute manuscripts for sales, donate copies of his books to libraries, autograph works for strangers, allow his name to be used on letterheads, supply personal information about himself, supply opinions on literary or other subjects.'

This was only partially successful; he then started getting letters from people wanting a copy of the card.

The columnist and critic, Alexander Woollcott, never took kindly to being interrupted when he was telling a story. At an old boys' reunion a classmate slapped him on the back when he was in the middle of a favourite anecdote and announced, 'Hello, Alex. You remember me, don't you?'

'I can't remember your name,' answered Woollcott, 'but don't tell me . . . ' before carrying on with his story.

When Groucho Marx was greeted in the same way his reply was characteristically to the point, 'I never forget a face, but I'll make an exception in your case.'

J M Barrie didn't enjoy being pestered at home. To a reporter who arrived unannounced on his doorstep and said cheerfully, 'Sir James Barrie, I presume?' he replied, 'You do,' and slammed the door in his face.

T E Lawrence may have had an ambivalent attitude to publicity but he took exception to celebrity hunters. At a cocktail party in Cairo during a period of intense heat, he was cornered by a lady of uncertain age, well known for pursuing the great and famous.

'Ninety-two, today, Colonel Lawrence! Imagine it, ninety-two,' she began with exaggerated gestures against the heat.

'Many happy returns madam,' replied Lawrence.

Viscount Whitelaw, or Willie Whitelaw as he then was, came a bit unstuck at a reception at the American Embassy. He'd got into conversation, a long one as it turned out, with a man whose face was vaguely familiar. They both shared a passion for golf, but after breaking off to talk to other people, Whitelaw asked a friend, 'Do tell me, who's that American I was talking to? He doesn't seem to have much sense of humour.'

'Bob Hope,' answered his friend.

There but for the grace of God goes Donald Sinden. I remember a press reception during the first week's work filming *The Cruel Sea*. Still new to this aspect of the business, I asked what I was expected to do. 'Talk about yourself, the film and the Rank Organization – in that order,' the publicity director told me. The trouble was no one in the room seemed the slightest bit interested when I entered, so I chose the prettiest girl there, introduced myself and started on my preordained script. After twelve minutes on myself, eight on the film and four on the Rankery I ran out of steam and asked my lovely companion which paper she worked for. 'I'm from the Rank Organization publicity department,' she said.

I was given another bit of advice at that time which

had much the same result. Les Norman, the producer of *The Cruel Sea*, had told me that I should behave more like a 'star', which seemed to amount to pushing my weight about and telling other people what to do. Back on the set I revelled in my newly won confidence, placed the chair emblazoned DONALD SINDEN in a prominent place and sat in it regally. Enter two electricians wanting to lay a cable where I was sitting. 'You can lay it over there,' I said imperiously

'F— you,' one of them replied. I stopped being a 'star' after that.

Robert Atkins, the actor and director, might have sympathized. He and the actor Ralph Truman were walking beside the docks in Bristol once when they came across a four-masted schooner. 'Look at her,' mused Atkins. 'That beautiful barque has sailed the seven seas bringing us tea from Ceylon, jewels from India, silks from China, spices from Samarkand and there she lies about to depart at our behest.' Then to one of the deckhands he called, 'Sailor! Whither sailest thou?'

Scarcely bothering to turn, the man answered back, 'Shag off.'

It was always the custom at Stratford-upon-Avon for the leading actor to read the lesson in Holy Trinity Church on the Sunday nearest Shakespeare's birthday. In 1945 Atkins was not asked. Extremely annoyed, he cornered Canon Prentice in the High Street. 'Can you adduce any cogent reason why *I* should not read the f— lesson?' The canon tried to explain that after all Atkins had read the lesson for the previous three years and he thought it time for a change. 'Well,' grumbled Atkins, 'you can stuff yer church and you can stuff yer steeple! – except of course the bells which I understand are the most melodious in Warwickshire.'

No doubt there are those would have felt just as outraged by a sign displayed beside a locked gate barring entry to the garden of one of London's more exclusive squares. 'Only the very smallest dogs, in charge of their owners, are allowed in these gardens off the leash,' it read. 'All other dogs, and all dogs in charge of servants, must be kept on the leash.'

F E Smith was in the habit of wandering into the Athenaeum Club to spend an unauthorized penny after lunch at the Café Royal, on his way back to the House of Lords. In the end a group of members persuaded the club secretary to tackle him one afternoon. 'Lord Birkenhead, are you a member of this club?' enquired the timorous man as F E emerged from the Gents.

Surveying the columns, marble staircase and fine paintings, he enquired, 'Oh, it's a club as well is it?'

Sir Henry Irving adopted a similar tactic in the Garrick Club, though unlike F E Smith he was on legitimate ground. A new member, anxious to claim Irving as an acquaintance approached with the greeting, 'Hello, Irving, an extraordinary thing has just happened to me. A total stranger stopped me in the street and said, "God bless me, is that you?"'

In his characteristic staccato Irving asked, 'And . . . er . . . was it?'

The first meeting between Jean Harlow and Margot Asquith didn't go any better. 'Margott,' said the blonde siren from Hollywood, 'how lovely to meet you.'

'My dear,' said Lady Asquith, 'the 'T' is silent – as in Harlow.'

The actress Beatrice Lillie and Mrs Armour, wife of the Chicago meat-packing tycoon, didn't actually meet in their celebrated encounter – but then they didn't need to. The setting was a beauty salon in the Windy City. Inside were Miss Lillie and several members of her company, on tour in a Chicago theatre. Mrs Armour, who arrived after them, didn't take kindly to being kept waiting and told the receptionist in the affected tones attributed to the recently rich, 'Oh, if I'd known all these theatrical people would be here today, I'd never have come.'

Having identified the owner of the voice, who was still waiting when she swept into the reception area on her way out, Miss Lillie told the receptionist in her most gracious English voice, 'You may tell the butcher's wife that Lady Peel has finished.'

In 1834 the anonymous author of *Hints on Etiquette and the Usages of Society, with a Glance at Bad Habits* offered this salutary example:

An unfortunate Clerk of the Treasury, who, because he was in the receipt of good salary, and being also a 'triton among minnows' of Clapham Common, fancied himself a great man, dined at the B—f S—k Club, where he sat next to a noble Duke, who, desirous of putting him at ease, conversed freely with him, yet probably forgot even the existence of such a person half-an-hour afterwards. Meeting his Grace in the street some days after, and encouraged by his previous condescension the hero of the quill, bent on claiming his acquaintance, accosted him in a familiar 'hail-fellow-well-met'-ish manner – 'Ah, my Lord, how d'ye do?' The Duke looked surprised. 'May I know, Sir, to whom I have the honour of speaking?' said his Grace, drawing up. 'Oh! why don't you know? We dined together at the B—k S—k Club the other evening! I'm MR TIMMS OF THE TREASURY!!' 'Then,' said the Duke, turning on his heel, 'MR TIMMS OF THE TREASURY, I wish you a *good morning.*'

I suspect I caused an equal measure of outrage on the one fishing trip I went on with my father-in-law. Ours was not an easy relationship and I had no interest in fishing, so the prospects for the stay on Loch Tay were not promising. However, to everyone's astonishment I caught a fifteen-pound salmon. It was the only fish either of us caught during the entire expedition and judging by the reaction of the other guests the only fish anyone had caught for a very long time.

On the way down to dinner on the evening of my triumph my father-in-law held me back on the stairs to survey the dining-room from above. We gave ourselves a couple of minutes to allow the other guests to be seated and then marched in to our table while twenty-six pairs of eyes followed us across the room.

I suppose for once I could have raised my esteem with my father-in-law. But it was not to be.

'I hear you caught a salmon – what were you using?' enquired the first visitor at our table.

'A bent pin on a piece of string,' I answered.

'This is no time to be facetious, young man,' he said as he stalked off.

I may have found a kindred spirit in Salvador Dali. He once took his pet ocelot into a New York restaurant and tied it to the table while he ordered a coffee. A middle-aged matron walking past spotted the animal and ask in horror, 'What's that?'

'It's only a cat,' replied Dali. 'I've painted it over with an op-art design.'

Relieved, but embarrassed at her reaction, the woman dared a closer look and said with relief, 'Now I can see what it is. At first I thought it was a real ocelot.'

Shortcomings over food, whether in quality or quantity, not infrequently get a tart response. Uncharacteristically for a Frenchman, Maurice Chevalier had a reputation for serving exquisite but minuscule portions. Most guests accepted this, but the novelist Jacqueline Susann was not among them. After dinner at Chevalier's country home, she and her husband were taken into their host's study and offered a drink. Declining this, she told him, 'Maurice, I never drink on an empty stomach.'

When Disraeli was guest of honour at a large public dinner the kitchens were so far from the banqueting hall that most of the food was cold by the time it reached the table. Sipping his champagne after the meal, Disraeli murmured, 'Thank God! I have at last got something warm.'

Robert Lutyens took his father, the architect Sir Edwin Lutyens, to lunch at the Garrick Club in order to ask whether he had any objections to his writing about him. Sir Edwin accepted the idea, but was less sanguine about the lunch. As the fish was served, he surveyed it seriously and then remarked, 'The piece of cod that passeth all understanding.'

George Bernard Shaw's vegetarianism didn't always find favour with his friends. On one occasion he was at a dinner party in London where his carnivorous neighbours were served something succulent and juicy while he was presented with a mixture of greens dressed with a variety of salad oils.

As he was about to tuck in, J M Barrie seated alongside, asked confidentially, 'Tell me one thing Shaw, have you eaten that or are you going to?'

When the artist James Whistler was in a restaurant in France he overheard an Englishman trying to order something to eat with considerable difficulty. 'May I help?' asked Whistler genially.

'Thank you,' replied the man crossly, 'but I can manage

perfectly well on my own.'

'I fancied contrary just now,' said Whistler, 'when I heard you desire the waiter bring you a dozen stairs.'

In addition to her obvious attributes Grace Kelly had a marvellous facility for languages. I discovered this during the filming of *Mogambo*, with Clark Gable and Ava Gardner, in which I was cast as the English husband of Grace, then a rising star in Hollywood. We first met in Nairobi, where Ava Gardner had all her meals sent up by room service, leaving Clark, Grace and me to dine together. Our waiter was a Kikuyu and when he appeared on the first evening to ask what we would like, Grace effortlessly ordered the entire meal in Swahili, which she had been swotting up on since she first learnt that the film was to be made in Kenya. After coffee had been served at the end of the meal, the waiter was slipping away when Grace asked him, '*Lete ndizi, tafadhali.*'

By that stage we had grasped that *lete* meant 'bring' and *tafadhali* 'please', but Clark, with some incredulity, asked her, 'What's an *ndizi* ?'

Before she could answer, the waiter turned and in a bored American accent answered, 'It's a banana,' and wearily made his way.

The main camp for the filming of *Mogambo* was on the Kagera River in Uganda, which was still a British colony. The Governor, Sir Andrew Cohen, had been out to spend a few days with us, sleeping in a special tent complete with armed guards and a Union Jack fluttering proudly outside. In return he invited some of us to stay with him at Government House in Entebee, idyllically situated above Lake Victoria. At the end of the meal Lady Cohen took Grace, Ava and the other ladies off and our host asked, 'Would anyone care to look at Africa by night?'

Outside the effect of the tropical night was magical.

The garden was lit by a full moon reflected in the mirror-like waters of the lake. Cicadas creaked in the shrubbery and the air was heavy with the scent of flowers. As I stood in wonderment I became aware of splashing sound. Looking round I saw the Governor and his entire staff happily peeing on the lawn!

The whole evening was redolent of Somerset Maugham, Kipling and every other author imbued with the traditions and ideals of our imperial past. The one person it was guaranteed not to impress was the film's director, John Ford. Steeped in a romanticized American view of his beloved Ireland, he seemed to blame me personally for all her ills and for the six months we worked together he didn't miss a chance to try to get the better of me, and every other Englishman he met.

Sir Andrew Cohen's invitation had of course been extended to the director. But at the last minute Ford claimed he was too busy to fly to Entebee with the rest of us. He followed later in his own aircraft and a car was kept waiting at the airport expressly to convey him to Government House.

We were having tea on the veranda, Ava and Grace wearing charming dresses, Clark and I appropriately dressed, I hope, when Ford arrived wearing creaseless baggy trousers, an ancient sports jacket, plimsolls and a baseball cap. His one concession to the occasion was a collar and tie, but the latter certainly would have been better left back at camp.

At six the Governor suggested that we might like to dress for dinner.

'Dress for dinner?' scoffed Ford. 'This is all I've brought with me!'

With only the briefest hesitation our host demurred, 'Very well, we will not dress for dinner.' Grace and Ava

had carefully brought enough clothes to cover any even-
tuality, Clark and I had brought the white dinner jackets
we wore on set and two of the Governor's staff who
joined us similarly attired had to slip out and return in
lounge suits. If it was a victory for John Ford, it was a
hollow one.

By this stage I had got used to his one-upmanship, but
in the early stages of our relationship it was very irksome.
Asked to join a game of Canasta, he asked, 'Do you play
Three or Five Canastas?'

'Three,' was the answer.

'I only play Five,' he said continuing on his way. If I'd
said 'Five', Ford's answer would predictably have been
'Three'.

On another occasion I was telling a few anecdotes of
The Cruel Sea when Ford joined us. I happened to men-
tion the American fleet in the English Channel and said,
'Their battleship the *Missouri* was anchored in Portland
Harbour . . . '

This gave Ford his cue, 'You said *the Missouri* – you
never say *the* when referring to a ship.'

'You're quite right,' I said and finished my story.

Now it was his turn with a naval anecdote during the
course of which he came out with the same misplaced
definite article when he referred to *the Missouri*.

'Aha! You said *the Missouri,*' I countered.

'In the States we say *the Missouri,*' he answered, trump-
ing me conclusively.

(It would have been interesting to see how John Ford
would have responded to another anecdote, set in Ireland
in the early 1920s. Dunsany Castle, the home of Lord
Dunsany in County Meath, was ransacked by a troupe of
Black and Tans. As they left the scene of destruction, his
Lordship's butler asked with unimpeachable Anglo-Saxon

sang-froid,'Who shall I say called?')

Too great an enthusiasm for what others have to say can be as much of an irritation at a dinner-party as Ford's desire to dominate. Dr Johnson was once put out by the unbridled laughter and ostentatious appreciation of everything he said displayed by a fellow guest at a small dinner-party in London. In the end he couldn't take any more and after a typical outburst, turned on the man to ask, 'Pray, sir, what is the matter? I hope I've not said anything that you can comprehend.'

(The Earl of Chesterfield, to whom Johnson sent a famously indignant letter when he offered his patronage *after* the publication of Johnson's great *Dictionary* in 1755, had this to say on the subject of laughter:

Having mentioned laughing, I must particularly warn you against it: and I could heartily wish that you may often be seen to smile, but never heard to laugh while you live. Frequent and loud laughter is the characteristic of folly and ill manners: it is the manner in which the mob express their silly joy at silly things; and they call it being merry. In my mind there is nothing so illiberal, and so ill-bred, as audible laughter. True wit, or sense, never yet made anybody laugh; they are above it: they please the mind, and give cheerfulness to the countenance. But it is low buffoonery, or silly accidents, that always excite laughter; and that is what people of sense and breeding should show themselves above. A man's going to sit down, in the supposition that he had a chair behind him, and falling down upon his breech for want of one, sets a whole company a laughing, when all the wit in the world would not do it; a plain proof, in my mind, how long and unbecoming a thing laughter is. Not to mention the disagreeable noise that it makes, and the shocking distortion of the face that it occasions. Laughter is easily restrained by a very little reflection; but, as it is generally connected with the idea of gaiety, people do not enough attend to its absurdity. I am neither of a melancholy, nor a cynical disposition; and am as willing, and as apt, to be pleased as anybody; but I am sure that, since I have had the full use of my reason, nobody has ever heard me laugh.)

And here is part of Johnson's letter, a better phrased put down it would be very hard to find:

Is not a Patron, my Lord, one who looks with unconcern on a man struggling for life in water, and, when he has reached ground, encumbers him with help? The notice which you have been pleased to take of my labours, had it been early, had been kind; but it has been delayed till I am indifferent, and cannot enjoy it; till I am solitary, and cannot impart it; till I am known, and do not want it.

Johnson was even-handed in his condemnation. A talkative woman who collared him one day, and of whom then he appeared to take little notice, broke off her monologue to ask, 'Why, Doctor, I believe you prefer the company of men to that of ladies.'

'Madam,' replied he, 'I am very fond of the company of ladies; I like their beauty, I like their delicacy, I like their vivacity, and I like their silence.'

Dorothy Parker was celebrated for nailing the loud-mouthed and opinionated. When a friend commented at a party that their hostess was very outspoken, she replied, 'By whom?'

A young man looking disdainfully round another New

York gathering said to her, 'I'm afraid I simply cannot bear fools.'

'How odd,' replied Miss Parker. 'Your mother could, apparently.'

The story is told of a husband and wife paying a visit to Paris at the time that Gladwyn Jebb was our ambassador there. A mutual friend had suggested that the visiting couple should telephone the Jebbs during their stay. This they did and were duly invited to lunch at the embassy. Five years later both couples were at a gathering in London and the visitor took the opportunity to introduce himself. 'I don't know whether you remember me, Lord Gladwyn, but when you were in Paris you very kindly invited us to lunch.'

'Oh,' answered the former ambassador, 'and did you come?'

J M Barrie had a disheartening experience when he dined with A E Housman in Cambridge. Barrie had been greatly looking forward to the meeting but when it came the two men found little to say to each other. Back in London and brooding on the disappointing outcome he wrote a note of apology, 'Dear Professor Houseman, I am sorry about last night, when I sat next to you and did not say a word. You must have thought I was a very rude man: I am really a very shy man. Sincerely yours, J M Barrie.'

'Dear Sir James Barrie,' began Housman's reply, 'I am sorry about last night, when I sat next to you and did not say a word. You must have thought I was a very rude man: I am really a very shy man. Sincerely yours, A E Housman. P S And now you've made it worse for you have spelt my name wrong.'

Shyness is one of the obstacles to be cleared by would-be fellows at both Oxford and Cambridge colleges, where dinner at high table is a testing time socially and intellectually. When C S Lewis was up for a fellowship at Magdalen College, Oxford, he was seated next to Sir Herbert Warren, the elderly and awesome president.

Sir Herbert remained completely silent throughout the first two courses. Only when the meat arrived did he ask, 'Do you like poetry, Mr Lewis?'

'Yes, President, I do,' replied the aspiring don.

As Sir Herbert didn't seemed inclined to pursue this line of conversation, Lewis added, 'I also like prose.' But that didn't elicit a response either and their meal ended as it had begun in total silence. In spite of this, or maybe because of it, Lewis was awarded his fellowship.

As a social activity eating can pose some awful dilemmas. I remember one particularly harrowing occasion that involved a pork chop. Once again I was filming on location, on the island of Barra in the Outer Hebrides. The film was *Rockets Galore*, a sequel to *Whisky Galore*, and after the day's work had ended we had the peaceful delights of the island at our disposal. The only drawback was the unrelenting diet of mutton, which in spite of the caterer's best endeavours brought the whole crew to the brink of mutiny as day after day on location we were faced with yet another unappetizing serving hopelessly disguised as something more alluring than it really was.

The day the pork chops arrived I found myself at the head of the queue when we broke for lunch. I suspect much of the perversity of the Arab personality can be put down to the total absence of pork and the predominance of mutton in their diet. The relief I felt that day strengthened my faith in Christianity. And for what I was about to receive the Lord made me truly thankful.

With the largest and most succulent chop safely on my

plate, accompanied by a dollop of mashed potato and a generous knob of butter, I hurried to one of the caravans where we ate our meals. Ahead of me was Jean Cadell, a matchless character actress who was also in the cast and, as it turned out, the mother of my agent-to-be. Jean, who was seventy-two at the time, was already seated when I bore in my lunch. 'Oh Donald,' she greeted me, 'how *sweet* of you!'

I hope my parents would have been proud of me as I handed her the tray; prouder still when I reached the caterer's van to find them heating up a batch of mutton for latecomers, now that all the pork chops had been spirited away.

I was reminded of this sad experience by a children's party held at the Palace of Westminster one Christmas. Among the adults joining in the fun was Margaret Thatcher who moved among the youngsters dishing out smiles and reproofs as the occasion demanded. Everyone was having a high old time, except for one small boy dissatisfied with what was on his dish. 'Miss, miss!' he hailed the passing prime minister. 'They've given me blancmange and I don't like blancmange!'

'That,' she told him, 'is what parties are all about: eating food you don't like!'

Judging by what he wrote in later life these stern values governed the home of the young G K Chesterton, though if his later girth is anything to go by, he experienced no such difficulties at mealtimes. At the age of three he had trouble getting his hat one day and screamed, after repeated efforts, 'If you don't give it to me, I'll say "AT"!'

When he looked back on those formative years Chesterton described the tenor of his home life as one in which 'nobody was any more likely to drop an "h" than to pick up a title.'

It's the chilling clarity with which children often see through what adults take for granted that can make conversations with them unnerving at times. I remember such an occasion with my eldest son, Jeremy. When he was seven we took him to see John Gielgud in *The Tempest*, Jeremy's first taste of Shakespeare. Knowing that we were coming round to his dressing-room after the performance John kept on his magnificent costume. Even when he offered Jeremy a chocolate, Prospero's spell remained unbroken and the chocolate was consumed while his parents chatted to Miranda's dad. When Jeremy did break his silence, though, he posed a question of such startling simplicity that it completely undermined the plot and would probably have stopped Shakespeare in his tracks if it had occurred to him. 'If you were so clever,' my son asked Prospero, 'why didn't you just magic yourself back to Italy?'

Marc's turn came over breakfast one morning when John Barton was staying with us during rehearsals for his epic production *The Wars of the Roses*. Marc was eight at the time and studying the Roman occupation of Britain, a subject on which John Barton is an acknowledged authority. 'When Vespasian defeated Caratacus,' he began, 'the actual site of the battle has never been established, but . . . '

'I know,' said Marc, 'but it's not Caratacus – it is Caractacus.'

Breakfast was not the best time of day to get into this and John Barton was not the right person to challenge. With the air of an indulgent schoolmaster he replied, 'No, Marc – Caratacus.'

'But it isn't,' Marc maintained, 'it is Caractacus.'

I could see the entire day's rehearsals being ruined by

this and having no knowledge of the subject, but immense respect for John's scholarship, I intervened, 'Marc, darling, I'm sure that Mr Barton is right.'

'No, he's not – it is Caractacus.'

This was too much for John who flew upstairs, returned immediately with a book and flicked through the pages as he entered. 'Yes – here we are! As I told you, it is C A R A oh dear . . . Yes. Well. You are perfectly right, Marc. I must go.' And off he went to rehearsal.

During a royal tour of Australia and New Zealand a couple of years after their marriage, the Prince and Princess of Wales were having a walk-about in South Australia when the Princess made for a group of young children and stopped to talk to them. She affectionately patted one little boy with tousled hair and asked, 'Why aren't you at school today?'

'I was sent home because I've got head lice,' he replied.

An episode a few years ago in a restaurant in Cowes raises a wry smile. It was summer. A party from a visiting yacht were dining ashore when a waiter caught his foot and tipped hot sauce down the back of one of the ladies. Quick off the mark her husband grabbed a jug of iced water and threw this over her. 'And they say the age of chivalry is dead!' remarked one of the other women.

Sir Thomas Beecham was travelling in a no-smoking compartment of a train, in the days when the Great Western railway was still in existence, when he was joined by a lady passenger. Having settled herself, his companion took out a cigarette and lit it, saying, 'I'm sure you won't mind.'

'Not at all,' said Beecham, 'provided that you don't mind if I'm sick.'

'I don't think you know who I am,' she retorted haughtily. 'I am one of the directors' wives.'

'Madam,' replied Beecham, 'if you were the director's only wife, I should still be sick.'

Played with greater skill and tact, that scene could have a very different outcome. Sir Winston Churchill's mother would have handled it better, if her experience on the political campaign trail is anything to go by. Lord Randolph Churchill's beautiful wife was canvassing for him in his Woodstock constituency and asked a workman in the street for his support.

'Not likely,' he answered. 'I'd never vote for a lazy bloke who doesn't leave his bed till dinner-time.'

Lady Churchill demurely told him that he was wrong on this detail at least, 'As I happen to be his wife, my evidence ought to be conclusive.'

'Lor' ma'am,' said the man, 'if you were my wife I should never want to get up.'

Others of her sex have favoured a more robust approach; Coral Browne for one. When she was rehearsing at the Haymarket Theatre once she came out of the stage door, found it pouring with rain, and had the luck to hail the only free taxi. At the same time, on the other side of the road, the same taxi was hailed by a respectable looking young man who had failed to see Miss Browne. Opening the door he said to the driver, 'Mansion House, please.'

'Sorry, sir,' replied the driver, 'but I saw the lady first.'

With no lady in sight along the rainswept street, the man asked, 'What lady?'

From the inner recesses of the taxi, where she sat swathed in furs, Coral Browne tapped her chest and growled in perfectly enunciated tones, 'This f— lady!'

One of the best Groucho Marx stories tells of the time when he was mistaken for the gardener. Down on his hands and knees in a flower bed, working with a trowel and sporting a pair of grubby trousers and an old sweat-shirt, he was spotted by a Beverly Hills matron prowling the neighbourhood for a new man to keep her own garden in shape.

'Oh gardener,' she called from the comfort of her Cadillac, 'how much does the lady of the house pay you a month?'

'Oh I don't get paid in dollars,' was the answer from the crouched figure. 'The lady of the house just lets me sleep with her.'

(It was probably a hostess of similar mien who received Groucho's farewell at the end of one of her gatherings, 'I've had a wonderful evening – but this wasn't it.')

Groucho's friend, the playwright George S Kaufman, also knew how to deflate the pompous. When a guest at one of the lunches Kaufman and others enjoyed at New York's Algonquin Hotel bored everyone rigid with a long-winded account of his family history, which he claimed he could trace right back to the Crusades, Kaufman inter-rupted, 'I had a famous ancestor, too. Sir Roderick Kaufman. He also went off to the Crusades . . . As a spy, of course.'

When Mark Twain was visiting this country he was the guest of the owner of an ancient house who took immod-erate pride in showing him its treasures. Pausing in front of a picture of the trial of Charles I, he pointed to an obscure clerk in the background and announced, 'An ancestor of mine.'

His guest, who like John Ford, couldn't stomach this sort of thing, pointed to one of the trial judges and said, 'An ancestor of mine but it is no matter, I have others.'

Gladstone took a liking to a seventeenth-century pic-ture of a Spanish nobleman handsomely decked out in plumes, ruffs and laced cuffs. But the price was too high in his opinion and, as the dealer was unwilling to budge, he left it behind.

Some time later he came across the portrait again, this time gracing the drawing-room of a wealthy businessman with whom he was dining. 'Do you like it?' asked his host, seeing Gladstone's interest. 'It's a portrait of one of my ancestors, a minister at the court of Queen Elizabeth.'

'Three pounds less and he would have been my ancestor,' replied Gladstone.

A guest whose grasp of history was no better lunched at the Sitwell family home, Renishaw Hall and happened to ask Edith Sitwell whether she remembered the house being built. Alice Keppel, who overheard this, quickly moved in and told him, 'My dear man, be careful! Not even the nicest girl in the world likes to be asked if she is four hundred years old.'

Other people's homes can rouse a mixture of emotions. Alexander Woollcott, seeing the country house and immaculately landscaped grounds recently acquired by the playwright Moss Hart, remarked, 'Just what God would have done if he had had the money.'

At about the same time the novelist Rex Stout was building a fourteen-room house with his own hands, on top of a hill in Danbury, Connecticut. When it was finished, he invited (perhaps unwisely) Frank Lloyd Wright to visit and give his opinion. The famous architect took his time looking round before commenting, 'A superb spot. Someone should build a house here.'

After enjoying a friend's hospitality to excess, Rex Whistler left the party and made his way down to the hall from where a loud crash seconds later confirmed that he wasn't really in fit shape to tackle the stairs. As he got to his feet, he asked tetchily who had designed the house.

'Norman Shaw,' said his host.

'I might have known it,' said Whistler. 'The damned teetotaller.'

Then there's Nancy Banks-Smith's observation, 'In my experience, if you have to keep the lavatory door shut by extending your left leg, it's modern architecture.'

What you find outside people's houses can be revealing – for those who have an eye to see. Covering a disturbance once at a university meeting, the *Daily Mirror* reported, 'It appears that the rumpus reached its climax when Lady Lewisham told the students: "Often I found that where Socialist voters lived there were dirty milk bottles on the doorstep."'

Outward appearances of every sort can be so significant. After his novel *The Green Hat* shot him to fame in the mid-1920s, Michael Arlen visited America. At Chicago he stepped off the train wearing a large hat and costly astrakhan overcoat and cutting an imposing figure. A waiting reporter asked him to what he attributed his artistic success. 'Per ardua ad astrakhan,' replied the author.

One place where stepping outside the conventional dress code was not a good idea was the Royal Enclosure at Ascot a century ago. Lord Harris tried this one year and didn't repeat the experiment. In place of the accepted morning coat or frock coat, he turned up sporting a bright tweed suit, which drew from the Prince of Wales the reproof, 'Mornin' Harris. Goin' rattin'?'

For wickedly funny royal put downs, the last word must surely belong to Elizabeth I who delivered this gem to the Earl of Oxford, as John Aubrey recorded it:

This earl of Oxford, making of his low obeisance to queen Elizabeth, happened to let a Fart at which he was so abashed that he went to travell seven years. At

his returne the queen welcomed him home and sayd,
'My lord, We have forgot the Fart.'

3

GUILTY PARTY

In life (and death) the law invariably has the last word.

As one who spent his formative years as anything but a regular habitué of the dock or the police cell, I found my one and only court appearance more than a trifle intimidating.

Circumstances were against me from the outset. Not only had I had been apprehended (with others) drinking intoxicating liquor after hours in a pub in Sheffield, coming from a staunch line of teetotallers that was tricky enough to explain, but with my poor wife ill and alone in an isolation hospital in Aberdeen, the image of a heartless blackguard was hard to shake off.

Having been advised to plead guilty, thereby saving the train fare and time spent travelling back to Sheffield for the hearing three months later, I must admit that this blot on my character had slipped from the forefront of my mind. It was only when the case made the headlines in the London *Evening Standard,* which Diana and I were perusing over a coffee on the Champs-Elysées that the enormity of what had happened fully dawned. The fact that we had each been fined three pounds did little to appease the disquiet of the family, and when we heard that the landlord looked likely to lose his licence because of the convictions we were advised to appeal and I found myself cast as defendant.

Our counsel, for we were defended together, had kindly arranged for me to give my evidence out of sequence as I had to be back in London for that evening's performance. In a court in Sheffield that didn't go down too well.

I didn't help my case when I took the oath, eschewing the printed card and declaiming; ' . . . The evidence I shall give shall be the truth, the whole truth and nothing but the truth – so help me God.' The last four words, I later gathered, owed more to my familiarity with Hollywood than the English legal system.

The prosecuting counsel was not a man I warmed to. The feeling, I suspect, was mutual. After eliciting from me my name and address, both of which he received with disdain, he enquired in what 'capacity' I had attended the 'party'.

Nervous and uncomprehending I paused and then asked him to repeat the question. This he did, patiently emphasizing each word as if to an imbecile, 'in what capacity did you attend the party?'

'In a perfectly sober one,' I answered truthfully, and for once with no intention to be funny. There too I misjudged. Laughter rose from the court and silence was called for. Things did not look good for my case when my counsel took to his feet.

'Mr Sinden; I understand you were guest at this party,' he enquired.

'Yes.'

'Did you pay for any drinks?'

'No.'

'Thank you Mr Sinden.'

My cross-examination was over. Our appeal now rested with our counsel, who then treated us to a masterly display of the finest points of the English adversarial system.

The next witness was a policeman, who stated in the course of his evidence that standing outside the pub he had heard yours truly announcing *inside* 'And I'll have a Guinness'. The policeman repeated almost word for word what he had said previously in the magistrates' court. But with Portia-like attention to detail our man was on his feet to challenge a tiny change in conjunction, a question of an 'if' or a 'but', but a difference all the same.

'Which is correct?' he demanded.

'What I said today – I have it written down.'

'Then how do you account for the discrepancy?'

'I can only imagine that it was taken down incorrectly at the magistrates' court – perhaps the shorthand stenographer misheard what I said.'

With that innocent remark the scales of justice imperceptibly teetered in our favour.

'And how far from you was the stenographer sitting?' demanded our counsel.

'About twelve feet.'

'About! You claim to be a police officer and you cannot be more accurate. I ask you again. How far away was the stenographer sitting?'

'I would say twelve feet,' answered the wretched policeman with anything but conviction.

'So you are stating that a stenographer sitting "you would say" – twelve feet from you "perhaps misheard what you said" in a quiet room, with no distractions – but you do not doubt what you say you heard through a *plate-glass* window!'

For the sake of a careless 'if' or a 'but' our appeal was allowed and in the eyes of the court, if not the universal agreement of the family, I returned to London a free man, my record unblemished.

My thoughts are taken back to that episode in Sheffield

when I consider a case brought before magistrates at the Thames Court concerning a suspected case of drunken driving. The policeman who had arrested the suspect told the court, 'He was unsteady on his feet, his breath smelt of alcohol and his eyes were glazed.'

'It was bound to be glazed,' shouted the witness, who took out his artificial right eye to reinforce his point.

'The other one was glazed too,' countered the policemen, but his confidence had gone and his case with it.

The Israeli statesman, Moshe Dayan, was well placed to adopt a similar ploy when he was stopped for speeding by a military policeman to whom he explained, 'I have only one eye. What do you want me to watch – the speedometer or the road?'

The tables were turned in another case in which the accused was suspected of indulging too liberally by a policeman whose own slow response suggested a fondness for the bottle as well.

'What exactly was the prisoner doing?' demanded the defence counsel.

'He was arguing with a taxi-driver,' answered the policeman ponderously.

'And you think that proves he was drunk?'

'No,' acknowledged the constable. 'But you see, there wasn't a taxi-driver there.'

Sir Edward Carson was more successful in demolishing a key prosecution witness in an Irish trial with just four questions, the first of which was, 'Are you a teetotaller?'

'No, I'm not.'

'Are you a moderate drinker?'

To this the witness gave no answer.

'Should I be right if I called you a heavy drinker?'

'That's my business.'

'Have you any other business?' asked Carson, return-ing to his seat triumphant.

During his time as a practising attorney, Abraham Lincoln relished the dramatic tension engendered by a well crafted cross-examination. As a young lawyer he examined a witness in a murder trial.

'You were with the murdered man just before, and saw the shooting?' asked Lincoln.

'Yes,' replied the witness.

'You stood near the two men?'

'Yes.'

'Was it in the open field?' 'Yes.'

'No; in the timber.'

'What kind of timber?'

'Beech timber.'

'The leaves of beech are rather thick in autumn?'

'Rather.'

'You could see the prisoner shoot?'

'Yes.'

'How near did this happen to the meeting place?'

'Three-quarters of a mile away.'

'Where were the lights?'

'Up by the minister's stand.'

'That was three-quarters of a mile away?'

'I have already said so.'

'Was there a candle where the prisoner was standing?'

'No. What would he want a candle for?'

'Then how did you see the shooting?'

'By moonlight.'

'You saw this shooting, at ten o'clock at night, in beech timber, three-quarters of a mile away from the lights? Saw the man point the pistol and fire? Saw it all by moonlight?'

'Yes, I have already said so.'

At this point Lincoln reached into a pocket and slowly

took out an almanac. Opening it carefully to the appropriate page, he then showed the court that on the night of the crime the moon had not been visible.

If anecdote and not attainment ensured preferment at the bar, F E Smith would still have risen to Lord Chancellor by the age of forty-seven. Accounts of his court-room exchanges are many; here are just a few.

F E once acted on behalf of a tram company which was in the delicate predicament of being taken to court by the parents of a small boy who had been knocked over and injured by one of its vehicles. The prosecution set out to prove that as a result of this accident the child could no longer raise one arm above his head and when he was called to give evidence the little boy presented a pathetic picture to the court.

Sensing the sympathy which the plaintive had aroused, F E was careful to ask questions in the a most encouraging and gentle manner. 'Your arm was hurt in this accident. Is that right?'

'Yes, sir.'

'And now you cannot lift your arm very high?'

'No, sir.'

'Do you think you could show the jury once more how high you can raise your arm since the accident?'

And with a brave effort the little boy lifted his arm until it was shoulder high and held it there for a moment so that the jury could see how painful it was.

'Thank you,' said F E kindly. 'And now could you show the jury how high you could raise it before the accident?'

Up shot the arm right above the boy's head.

Judges were not spared the future Lord Chancellor's stinging wit. On two celebrated occasions Judge Willes came off the worst from exchanges with F E Smith. 'You are extremely offensive, young man,' he told the young barrister crossly. To which he received the reply, 'As a matter of fact, we both are, and the only difference between us is that I am trying to be and you can't help it.'

Some time later they met again in court and in the course of the trial the judge enquired, 'What do you suppose I am on the bench for, Mr Smith?'

'It is not for me to attempt to fathom the inscrutable workings of Providence,' was F E's reply.

Mr Justice Ridley didn't fare much better. At the start of a trial he commented, 'Well, Mr Smith, I have read the pleadings and I don't think much of your case.'

'Indeed,' answered F E, 'I'm sorry to hear that m'lud, but your lordship will find that the more you hear it, the more it will grow on you.'

At Oxford F E Smith had been awarded one of the best firsts of his year and he was keenly disappointed when he was only awarded a second when he took a BCL as his second degree. Years later the professor who had given him the lower class after the oral part of his examination was refused silk by the then Lord Birkenhead. Always happy to settle an old score, F E explained, 'Silk is only awarded to academic lawyers of distinction.'

It was F E Smith's quickness of mind that more often than not caused these run-ins with his superiors on the bench. Before the Court of Appeal once he took great care to explain his case in the simplest terms, which inevitably took longer than it might otherwise have done. The Master of the Rolls took exception to the barrister's long-windedness and interrupted tartly, 'Really, Mr Smith, do give this court credit for some little intelligence.'

'That is the mistake I made in the court below, my lord,' answered F E before continuing with his carefully worded plea.

Across the Atlantic, the American attorney Max Steuer overstepped decorum and had to apologize to a judge whom he had offended, though even here he was able to gain the upper hand in stating, 'Your Honour is right and I am wrong, as your Honour generally is.' (It was Max Steuer who at the start of his cross-examination of a barber was informed loftily by the witness that he was 'a tonsorial artist'. 'Isn't that splitting hairs?' answered the attorney.)

Sniping such as this is not restricted to trial proceedings. Following a case in which Sir Edward Carson had been acting, the trial judge commented to him quietly on the marked discrepancy between two witnesses he had called. One, a carpenter, had given his evidence clearly, with conviction and to the complete satisfaction of the court. The other, a publican, had been rambling, contradictory and totally unconvincing in the dock. How could Carson explain this, the judge wanted to know. He couldn't, but simply observed it to be, 'Yet another case of the difference between bench and bar.'

Of course, judges were barristers themselves. Old habits die hard and barristers certainly don't have things all their own way.

Lord Ellenborough, presiding over a trial in which the defence counsel was young, inexperienced and terribly nervous, was devastating.

'My lord,' began the young barrister, 'my unfortunate client . . . my lord, my unfortunate client . . . my lord . . . my unfortunate client . . . my lord, my . . .

'Continue, sir, continue,' the judge told him, 'as far as you have proceeded hitherto, the court is entirely with you.'

When Mr Justice McCardie was elevated to the bench he invited a large number of fellow lawyers to celebrate his success. When his time came to speak, the new judge told his audience, 'I am especially glad to see here tonight those hundred solicitors each of whom sent me my first brief.'

Other judges are sparing with their words. Mr Justice Avory was one of these. He it was who earned the nickname The Acid Drop for his unbending manner and his habit of sitting impassively and silent throughout a trial, only to sum up with a few words spoken by lips that scarcely moved. Though even this minimal activity was enough to inspire one small child in a public gallery to exclaim excitedly, 'Daddy, Daddy – it's alive!'

Occasionally Avory would be a little more forthcoming, though his form of address was always intimidating. Questioning a witness, he demanded to know, 'You have been convicted before, haven't you?'

The man admitted he had, 'But it was due to the incapacity of my counsel rather than to any fault of my own.'

'It always is and you have my sincere sympathy,' replied Avory drily.

'And I deserve it,' the witness retorted, 'seeing that you were my counsel on that occasion.'

Sir William Grant, a former Master of the Rolls, shared Avory's penchant for silence in court, though this was tempered by a degree of patience that Avory never aspired to. For two days Sir William sat listening as an elaborate case was laid before the court, the crux of which was a particular interpretation of an Act of Parliament. Allowing the counsel to follow this course to the point when he had done full justice to his line of argument, Grant allowed himself the comment, 'Gentlemen, the Act on which the pleading has been found is repealed.'

In contrast was Lord Bramwell who was not a judge in

favour of prolonged submissions, particularly when they detained the court beyond the normal hour for adjournment. He once presided over a case in which a farmer had taken a pot shot at a boy stealing apples from his orchard. The case was simple but the defence counsel made a meal of his final appeal to the jury. The judge's summing up was more succinct. 'I shall leave the case to you in eight words,' he told the jury. 'The prisoner aimed at nothing and missed it.'

Lord Darling would have approved of this. He once listened to a defence counsel extolling his client's reputation which was unblemished but for one crime, in the counsel's words, 'a slight case of murder'.

Darling was not impressed. 'Unfortunately I have sentenced to death too many persons who bore the highest character to enable me to give that argument more than its due weight.'

Judges have sometimes been accused of too little familiarity with everyday life. In this respect Lord Darling was a telling example. Enquiring of one barrister, 'And who is George Robey?' he was informed, 'He is the Darling of the music halls, my lord.'

When another barrister referred in his submission to the Coliseum, Darling asked, 'Isn't that the place where the Christians feed the lions?'

'I think your lordship must be referring to the Trocadero,' was the polished reply, 'where Lyons feed the Christians.'

Several years ago, a county court in Surrey was treated to an interesting case of hit-and-run. The plaintiff told the court that he had been crossing a street in Guildford when a cow came charging round a corner, knocked him off his feet, trampled over him and carried on its way. In their defence, the owners of the cow claimed that the person in charge of a tame animal was not responsible for damage done by it which was 'foreign to its species'. Their counsel explained to the court that he would prove the cow had attacked the plaintiff, thereby absolving the owners of any liability. At this stage the judge stopped him to ask, 'Is one to abandon every vestige of common sense in approaching this matter?'

'Yes, my lord,' said the counsel.

The same question might have been asked by the judge in a trial of double-wife murder had the trial taken place in an English court of law. As it happened the case was heard in France where the cultural differences between our two nations were strikingly revealed.

The case concerned a Parisian who admitted killing his first wife because of her perpetual habit of undercooking his steak. Taking the plunge a second time he had chosen a bride who erred to the opposite extreme and always presented him with steaks *bien cuits*. After twelve years of this he had had enough and she went the way of her predecessor. After hearing all the evidence the judge cleared the defendant of murder and sentenced him to eight years for manslaughter on the grounds that 'the quality of the cooking is an important part of marriage'.

The law as it concerns marriage has aroused powerful emotions. Lord Chief Justice Russell offered a novel verdict when he was asked what was the penalty for bigamy. 'Two mothers-in-law,' he answered without hesitation.

At the end of a trial of bigamy in the last century, before the long overdue reform of divorce law in England, Mr Justice Maude used his summing up to deliver a scathing attack on the iniquity of the legislation as it then was. Before sentence was passed, the prisoner was asked if there were any mitigating circumstances for his action. He replied, 'My Lord, my wife took up with a hawker and ran away five years ago; and I have never seen her since, so I married this other woman last winter.'

'Prisoner at the bar,' began Maude, 'I will tell you what you ought to have done, and if you say you did not know, I will tell you that the Law conclusively presumes that you did. You ought to have instructed your attorney to bring action against the hawker for criminal conversation with your wife. That would have cost you about one hundred pounds. When you had recovered substantial damages against the hawker, you would have instructed your attorney to sue in the ecclesiastical courts for a divorce *a mensa et toro*. That would have cost you £200 or £300 more. When you had obtained a divorce *a mensa et toro*, you would have had to appear by counsel before the House of Lords for divorce *a vinculo matrimonii*. The bill might have been opposed in all its stages in both Houses of Parliament, and altogether you would have had to spend about £1,000 or £1,200. You will probably tell me that you never had 1,000 farthings of your own in the world, but, prisoner, that makes no difference. Sitting here as a British judge, it is my duty to tell you that this is not a country in which there is one law for the rich and another for the poor.'

The outcome of a more recent case of breach-of-promise was happier. The action was brought by a Miss Week against a Mr Day but before it reached court they patched up their differences and became engaged after all. When this was announced in open court Frank Lockwood (later to become Solicitor-General), who had been due to represent the plaintiff, scribbled down this brief summary of what had happened and passed it to the judge:

> One Day the more, one Week the less,
> But we must not complain.

There'll soon be little Days enough
To make a Week again.

What a pity more disputes within families can't be reconciled as easily.

Tracing my forebears, as opposed to their feuds both in and out of the law, has long been an absorbing hobby of mine, and one that introduced me to the treasures of the Public Records Office. So often did I visit it in carrying out my research that I began to find my way around and one day made an exciting discovery. A polished oak display case caught my attention. Through the thick glass I could make out the last part – I counted nine lines – of an old document with a name at the end which made me stop in my tracks. It was William Shakespeare's signature at the foot of his will. I subsequently learned that his will was stored in that showcase with those Milton, Lord Nelson and the Duke of Wellington.

Some time later I chanced to be in the Public Records Office continuing to track down my ancestors when a senior member of staff who had always given me expert help, came over to my desk. They were about to take some publicity photographs and would I mind appearing in some as a typical researcher? I was happy to oblige and concluded that my acting ability would not be overstrained in presenting a calm researcher, engrossed in his task. As the photographer was checking his light meter, the member of staff returned and put a document before me suggesting that it might be of interest to me. I doubt if they were ever able to use the first photograph which was taken just as I discovered that I was holding Shakespeare's will.

Very carefully I touched his signature. I still recall that feeling of excitement when I read the words above it.

We might reasonably expect it to throw light on his marriage to Anne Hathaway but the evidence is inconclusive. What are we to make of his bequest to her of 'me second best bed'? Who deserved his best bed? I think it was John Barton who told me that the second best bed would have been associated with a married couples' domestic life and therefore the bequest would have been quite romantic. If this were the case then we might have expected to read some lines of tribute to Anne, but there are none.

It is also noteworthy that the will makes no mention of the tools of his trade or his literary works. What happened to them? As so often, Shakespeare's words raise more questions than they answer.

The playwright Eugene O'Neill wrote a will with the definite intention of cheering up his wife, Carlotta. The family's pet dog, Blemie, was dying of old age and O'Neill penned 'Blemie's Will'.

I, Silverdene Emblem O'Neill (familiarly known to my family, friends and acquaintances as Blemie), because the burden of my years and infirmities is heavy upon me, and I realize the end of my life is near, do hereby bury my last will and testament in the mind of my Master. He will not know it there until after I am dead. Then, remembering me in his loneliness, he will suddenly know of his treatment, and I ask him then to inscribe it as a memorial to me.

I have little in the way of material things to leave. Dogs are wiser than men. They do not set great store upon things, they do not waste their days hoarding property. They do not ruin their sleep worrying about how to keep the objects they have not. There is nothing of value I have to bequeath except my love and my faith. These I leave to all those who have loved me, to my Master and mistress; who I know will mourn me most, to Freeman who has been so good to me, to Cyn and Roy and Willie and Naomi and – but if I should list all those who have loved me it would force my Master to write a book. Perhaps it is vain of me to boast when I am so near death; which returns all beasts and vanities to dust; but I have always been an extremely loveable dog.

I ask my Master and Mistress to remember me always, but not to grieve for me too long. In my life I have tried to be a comfort to them in time of sorrow, and a reason for added joy in their happiness. It is painful for me to think that even in death I should cause them pain. Let them remember that while no dog has ever had a happier life (and this I owe to their love and care for me), now that I have grown blind and deaf and lame; and even my sense of smell fails me so that a rabbit could be right under my nose and I might not know, my pride has sunk to a sick, bewildered humiliation. I feel life is taunting me with having over-lingered my welcome. It is time I said goodbye, before I become too sick a burden on myself and on those who love me. It will be a sorrow to leave them, but not a sorrow to die. Dogs do not fear death as men do. We accept it as part of life, not as something alien and terrible which destroys life. What may come after death, who knows? I would like to believe with those of my fellow Dalmatians who are devout Mohammedans, that there is a Paradise where one is always young and full-bladdered; where all the day one dillies and dallies with an amorous multitude of houris, beautifully spotted; where jack rabbits that run fast but not too fast (like the houris) are as the sands of the desert; where each blissful hour is mealtime; where in long evenings there are a million fireplaces with logs forever burning, and one curls oneself up and blinks into the flames and nods and dreams, remembering the old brave days on earth, and the love of one's Master and Mistress.

I am afraid this is too much for even such a dog as I am to expect. But peace, at least, is certain. Peace and long rest for weary old heart and head and limbs, and eternal sleep in the earth I have loved so well. Perhaps after all, this is best.

One last request I earnestly make. I have heard my Mistress say, 'When Blemie dies we must never have another dog. I love him so much I could never love another one.' Now I would ask her, for love of me, to have another. It would be a poor tribute to my memory never to have a dog again. What I would feel is that, having once had me in the family, now she cannot live without a dog! I have never had a narrow jealous spirit. I have always held that most dogs are good (and one cat, the black one I have permitted to share the living-room rug during the evenings, whose affection I have tolerated in a kindly spirit, and in rare sentimental moods, even reciprocated a trifle). Some dogs, of course, are better than others. Dalmatians, naturally, as everyone knows, are best. So I suggest a Dalmatian as my successor. He can hardly be as well bred or as well mannered or as distinguished and handsome as I was in my prime. My Master and Mistress must not ask the impossible. But he will do his best, I am sure, and even his inevitable defects will help by comparison to keep my memory green. To him I bequeath my collar and leash and my overcoat and raincoat, made to order in 1929 at Hermès in Paris. He can never wear them with the distinction I did, walking around the Place Vendôme, or later along Park Avenue, all eyes fixed on me in admiration; but again I am sure he will do his utmost not to appear a mere gauche provincial dog. Here on the ranch, he may prove himself quite worthy of comparison, in some respects. He will, I presume, come closer to jack rabbits than I have been able to in recent years. And, for all his faults, I hereby wish him the happiness I know will be his in my old home.

One last word of farewell, dear Master and Mistress. Whenever you visit my grave, say to yourselves with regret but also with happiness in your hearts at the remembrance of my long happy life with you: 'Here lies one who loved us and whom we loved.' No matter how deep my sleep I shall hear you, and not all the power of death can keep my spirits from wagging a grateful tail.

The stage, of course, has long offered the chance to take on a different role or persona. It has often been suggested that some actors are only tolerable when they are acting a part other than the one given them in life. One odd will shows that it is not just actors who are attracted to the new lives possible on stage. When he died in 1955, Juan Potomachi bequeathed part of his fortune to the Teatro Dramatico in Buenos Aires, but with an unusual condition. His will states:

All my life I wanted to be on the stage. Lack of talent prevented me at first from realizing that wish. Later my position in the community as a prominent businessman barred me altogether from the stage.

I leave 200,000 pesos to a fund from which talented young actors shall get yearly scholarships. My only condition is that my head be preserved and used as a skull in Hamlet.

My dearest wish would be fulfilled after all, as I would still have a part in a play after my death.

That Señor Potomachi was not alone in having such a wish is seen in a nineteenth-century will. John Reed had been a stagehand for forty-four years at a theatre in Philadelphia. Mourners after his death were taken aback by the following clause in his will, 'my head to be separated from my body immediately after my death; the latter to be buried in a grave; the former, duly macerated and prepared, to be brought to the theatre where I have served all my life, and to be employed to represent the skull of Yorick in the play *Hamlet.*'

Probably it is just as well that neither will insisted that the preserved heads should be used at the close of *Macbeth* when the head of the vanquished tyrant, freshly severed in the fight with Macduff, is held up for inspection.

Generations of trainee priests in a seminary outside Rome had reason to enjoy the special provision made for them in the eleventh-century will of Johann Fugger. This German bishop, finding that he had to travel to Rome, had the foresight to send his steward ahead of him to find the best taverns along the route. The steward had been asked to write the word *Est* ('It is' in Latin) above the doors of the inns that served the best wine and following this welcome trail of three-letter words the bishop made his way southwards. Just north of Rome he came to the small town of Montefascione where he found an inn bearing the enthusiastic classification *Est! Est! Est!* So good was the wine served here that Fugger drank it for the rest of his life and arranged on his death to be buried in the town. A further wish contained in his will was carried out each year when a barrel of the local wine was poured over his grave. Time passed. Bishop Fugger drifted into distant memory and the needs of the living took on a growing importance to the extent that one year the wine was no longer poured into the bishop's grave, but was sent to the local seminary for the enjoyment of the young priests.

A seventeenth-century community of French monks became curiously connected with a will that was to have unexpected consequences. The will in question was that of a courtesan, Ninon de Lenclos. As one who liked to keep her affairs in order, this good lady kept records of all her relationships and when confined to the monastery seduced 439 monks in quick order. History does not dwell on the effect this had on the monks but it did no harm to Mlle Lenclos who lived well into her eighties. In her will she devoted only a modest sum to cover her funeral expenses but left a thousand francs to the young son of her attorney, M Arouet. Such encouragement was aptly rewarded; the boy became better known as Voltaire.

The earlier French writer, Rabelais, was matter of fact in disposing of his worldly goods. 'I owe much,' read his will, 'I possess nothing. I give the rest to the poor.'

To return to Mlle Lenclos, or one of her American 'sisters', for a moment. The will of Kate Vandenberg cheerfully answers the question posed in the requiem 'Death where is they sting?'

Kate was a lady of the town. To quote the son of her attorney who drew up her will, 'Everybody in town knew what she was, though of course some of the men knew better than others.'

The attentions of one man, however, were less to her liking. This was a rabid reformer who after years of campaigning against her was elected mayor on a ticket to clean up the town and clean up Kate in particular. Her death shortly after his victory robbed him of his opportunity, but it presented her with hers. In her will Kate Vandenberg left a small bequest 'to one who had long been her valued friend' – the mayor.

A different class of endowment features in the will of Robert Louis Stevenson. A young friend of the family had a Christmas Day birthday and complained to the author that she always missed out on one set of presents. After his death she discovered that he had left her his own birthday, there was one proviso, 'if, however, she fails to use this bequest properly, all rights shall pass to the President of the United States.'

A similar spirit of generosity inspired one Jack Luke whose death in 1812 led to every child who attended his funeral receiving a penny (over seven hundred showed up). In addition every woman in the village was given a shilling and the bell ringers each received half a guinea, to 'strike off one peal of grand bobs' at the exact moment of his burial. His last bequest was for forty dozen penny loaves to be thrown from the church steeple at noon every Christmas Day thereafter.

Paignton in Devon is the subject of a more circumspect bequest which provides for the baking of gigantic plum pudding weighing over three hundred pounds, to be divided among needy families. This happens once every fifty years, however, and the next portions are not to be handed out until 2001.

This preoccupation with sustenance when contemplating the great hereafter took an even more bizarre turn in the case of a lady from Philadelphia, who passed away in 1913. Her will appeared in her handwritten recipe book under the heading 'Chili Sauce Without Working':

4 quarts of ripe tomatoes, 4 small onions, 4 green peppers, 2 teacups of sugar, 2 quarts of cider vinegar, 2
ounces ground allspice, 2 ounces cloves, 2 ounces cin-
namon, 12 teaspoonfuls salt. Chop tomatoes, onions
and peppers fine, add the rest mixed together and bottle cold. Measure tomatoes when peeled. In case I die
before my husband I leave everything to him.

The two daughters of a wealthy ninetenth-century
Scotsman by the name of McAllister each received her
weight in one-pound notes according to the provisions of
their father's will. The canny Scotsman while appearing
scrupulously fair, evidently favoured the better endowed
of his offspring – the one who inherited the best of fifteen
thousand pounds more than her sister.

In some ways having little or nothing to leave behind
saves so many problems. Rabelais's was one solution;
more long-winded, but a good deal more entertaining was
that adopted by a New York singing teacher who went to
meet his maker in 1965 with little to his name but a good
nature and cheerful disposition. This was his will:

1. I direct that all my creditors be paid except my landlord.
2. I give and bequeath to my good friend, Theodore
   Weber, my best aluminium tin if I die of anything
   but indigestion. In that event I give him a sad
   farewell.
3. To my old friend, Ann Lewis, I give and bequeath
   Purcell's 'Passing By', which I wrongfully took and
   carried away last Christmas.
4. I give and bequeath to my dear friend, Mrs George
   Hale, the satisfaction of being remembered in my
   will.

5. To my old pal, Mary Ledgerwood, I give and bequeath the sum of 35 cents. It's not much but it's the beginning of a Scotch fortune.

6. I leave to my lawyer, Huber Lewis, the task of explaining to my relatives why they didn't get a million dollars apiece.

7. I appoint Huber Lewis executor of my will. In view of his profession, I suppose we had better require him to furnish a bond. I give him full power to sell, mortgage or pledge any or all of my estate for the purpose of paying the legacy left by Article 5, and if sufficient sum cannot be realized, I warn him to be wary of the legatee.

His will then broke into a personal version of a familiar Gilbert and Sullivan refrain which heralded the signatures of his witnesses:

Three little maids from school are we
Called to witness this will, you see,
And testify to its propriety
Three little maids from school.
Everything has been properly done,
The testator's books suggested a 'bun',
But he knew right enough we considered it fun,
Three little maids from school.

If his music lessons were conducted in the same spirit, what a loss his pupils must have felt.

When the fourth Earl of Pembroke died in 1650 he left a will cast in a similarly entertaining mould:

I, Philip, IV Earl of Pembroke and Montgomery, being, as I am assured, of unsound health, but of sound memory – as I well remember me that five years ago I did vote for the despatching of old Canterbury, neither have I forgotten that I did see my King upon the scaffold – yet as it is said that death doth even now pursue me, and, moreover, as it is yet further said that it is my practice to yield under coercion, I do make my last will and testament.

Imprimis: As for my soul, I do confess I have often heard men speak of my soul, but what may be these same souls, or what their destination, God knoweth; for myself, I know not.

Men have likewise talked to me of another world, which I have never visited, nor do I even know an inch of the ground that leadeth thereto. When the King was reigning, I did make my son wear a surplice, being desirous that he should become a Bishop, and for myself I did follow the religion of my master; then came the Scotch, who made me a Presbyterian, but since the time of Cromwell, I have become an Independent. These are, methinks, the three principal religions of the Kingdom – if any of the three can save a soul, I desire they will return it to Him who gave it to me.

. . . put not my body beneath the church-porch for I am, after all, a man of birth, and I would not that I should be interred there, where Colonel Pride was born.

Item: I give my two best saddle-horses to the Earl of Denbigh whose legs, methinks, must soon begin to fail him. As regardeth my other horses, I bequeath them to Lord Fairfax, that when Cromwell and his council take away his commission he may still have some horse to command.

Item: I give nothing to my Lord Saye, and I do make him this legacy willingly, because I know that he will faithfully distribute it unto the poor.

Item: Seeing that I menace a certain Henry Mildmay, but did not thrash him, I do leave the sum of fifty pounds sterling to the lacquey that shall pay unto him my debt.

Item: I bequeath to Thomas May, whose nose I did break at a mascarade, five shillings. My intention had been to give him more; but all who shall have seen his 'History of the Parliament' will consider that even this sum is too large.

Item: I give to the Lieutenant-General Cromwell one of my words, the which he must want, seeing that he hath never kept any one of his own.

Item: I give up the ghost.

Lord Chesterfield, who in life rarely shrank from dishing out advice, especially to his unfortunate godson, made sure that the same heir should be rendered 'unfortunate' in a more coldly practical way after his death, if temptation should get the better of him with his ever-watchful godfather removed from the scene:

. . . in case my said godson Philip Stanhope shall at any time hereafter keep, or be concerned in the keeping of, any racehorse or racehorses, or pack or packs of hounds, or reside one night in Newmarket, that infamous seminary of iniquity and ill-manners during the course of the races there, or shall resort to the said races, or shall use in any one day at any game or bet whatsoever the sum of £500, then, and in any cases aforesaid, it is my express Will, that he my said Godson shall forfeit and pay out of my estate the sum of £5000 to and for the use of the Dean and Chapter of Westminster, for every such offence and misdemeanor as is above specified, to be recovered by action for debt in any of his Majesty's Courts of Record at Westminster.

Perhaps a greater degree of sympathy might go to the child of a Yorkshire priest who, in 1804, threatened to cut her out of his will on these grounds:

Seeing that my daughter Anna has not availed herself of my advice touching the objectionable practice of going about with her arms bare up the elbows, my will is that, should she continue after my death in this violation of the modesty of her sex, all the goods, chattels, moneys, land, and other that I have devised to her for the maintenance of her life shall pass to the oldest of the sons of my sister Caroline.

Should anyone take exception to this my wish as being too severe, I answer that licence in dress in a woman is a mark of a depraved mind.

Other testators have used their wills to broadcast in death what they kept secret in life. A bequest of £50 a year to the bell ringers of Bath Abbey was made a century ago by a certain Colonel Charles Nash. His was not a happy marriage. The conditions he laid down in his will were that the bells should be rung in his memory between the hours of eight in the morning and eight in the evening of two days of the year. On the anniversary of his wedding the bells were to be rung 'with doleful accentuation' but to celebrate his release from his marriage the bells were to be rung 'with a merry peal' on the anniversary of his death.

John Davis, yet another disgruntled husband, left his wife with a mere five shillings as, 'It is sufficient for her to get drunk for the last time at my expense.' That least

made it clear which of the lady's faults was being target-
ed, but as a general condemnation of marital disharmony
few wills can beat one from New Jersey which stated, 'To
my wife Anna (who is no damn good) I leave one dollar.'

In the case of the German poet, Heinrich Heine, possible faults in his wife remained for later discovery. He left
her all his estate provided that she remarried '. . . because
then there will be at least one man who will regret my
death.' The other side of the coin was revealed in the will
of a wealthy French merchant who bequeathed a substantial sum to the woman who had rejected him twenty
years earlier. He wanted to thank her for, 'a happy bachelor life of independence and freedom'.

For damning dismissals, however, few wills can match
that of a successful industrialist who died in Philadelphia
in 1947 leaving the following:

To my wife I leave her lover, and the knowledge that I
wasn't the fool she thought I was.

To my son I leave the pleasure of earning a living.
For twenty-five years he thought the pleasure was
mine. He was mistaken.

To my daughter I leave $100,000. She will need it.
The only piece of business her husband ever did was to
marry her.

To my valet I leave the clothes he has been stealing
from me for ten years. Also the fur coat he wore last
summer while I was in Palm Beach.

To my chauffeur, I leave my cars. He almost ruined
them and I want him to have the satisfaction of finish-
ing the job. To my partner, I leave the suggestion that
he take some clever man in with him at once if he
expects to do any business.

4

OFF THE RECORD

'In politics,' observed Clare Boothe Luce, the American writer, politician and diplomat, 'women type the letters, lick the stamps, distribute the pamphlets and get out the vote. Men get elected.'

Nancy Astor might have disagreed on this last point, but she knew all about combating the male preserve in establishing her own parliamentary career, which climaxed when she became the first woman to take a seat in the House of Commons. During an election meeting in her first campaign in Plymouth a man shouted from the audience, 'Your husband's a millionaire, ain't he?'

'I should certainly hope so,' his future MP shouted back, 'that's why I married him.'

At another meeting, another heckler (a woman this time), bellowed, 'My children are as good as yours.'

'As which of mine?' was the instant response. 'I've got some worse than any of yours – but I might have one who was better.'

Even when elected Nancy Astor still had difficulty establishing her credentials with the general public. Spotting a young American sailor in Parliament Square admiring the Palace of Westminster, she asked him whether he would like to go inside.

'You're the sort of broad my mother told me to avoid,' he answered, hurrying on his way.

Inside the House she was inclined to interrupt other speakers more than was customary, even in the Commons. When one of her victims rounded on her she claimed to have been listening for ages before opening her mouth. 'Yes, we've *heard* you listening,' said her infuriated opponent.

A greater source of annoyance to many of her colleagues was Nancy Astor's conviction that she had no need to prove herself equal to them, since the female of the species was quite simply the superior sex. 'I married beneath me, all women do,' was her maxim.

Other politicians have turned such entrenched views to their advantage. After Sir Robert Menzies had been sworn in as Prime Minister of Australia, a reporter from one of the country's left-wing papers asked bluntly, 'I suppose, Mr Prime Minister, that you will consult the powerful interests that control you in choosing your cabinet.'

'Young man, keep my wife's name out of this,' answered Lady Menzies's husband.

It was while he was addressing a local political meeting that a woman heckler shouted, 'I wouldn't vote for you if you were the Archangel Gabriel!'

'If I were the Archangel Gabriel,' replied Menzies, 'you would scarcely be in my constituency.'

The campaign trail and public meetings are to the politician what the rehearsal room is to the actor – with some exceptions. Actors are spared Adlai Stevenson's assessment of canvassing – 'you have to kiss an awful lot of babies and shake an awful lot of hands and you sometimes wonder what they've shaken before.'

Clashes on the hustings help politicians hone their debating technique. 'Vote for you! I'd rather vote for the devil,' a heckler yelled at Disraeli in his early days. 'Quite so,' replied the politician, allowing himself a momentary pause before continuing, 'and if your friend is not standing?'

Here's Harold Laski's quelling of a heckler at a public meeting in more recent times, 'Yes, my friend, we are both Marxists, you in your way, I in Marx's.'

Such exchanges prepare you for the unexpected too. Theodore Roosevelt, whom it was generally unwise to heckle, was once greeted by the slightly boozy cry from the floor, 'I am a Democrat!'

'May I ask the gentleman why he is a Democrat?' enquired Roosevelt, leaning over the lectern and smiling indulgently.

'My grandfather was a Democrat, my father was a Democrat, and I am a Democrat.'

'My friend, suppose your grandfather had been a jackass, and your father had been a jackass, what would you be?'

'A Republican!' rang out the triumphant reply.

Among Roosevelt's Republican successors in the White House, Ronald Reagan could draw on both acting and political experience in his campaigning. Hemmed in by a crowd of angry students brandishing placards and chanting, 'We are the future,' Reagan chose to reply by scribbling on a scrap of paper which he held to the inside of the window for their inspection. 'I'll sell my bonds,' it read.

Even Reagan's opponents acknowledged his success in getting across his message, particularly on television. In his first budget address he used a handful of small change to explain the current value of the dollar. 'It takes an actor to do that,' a Democrat grudgingly remarked. 'Carter would have emphasized all the wrong words. Ford would have fumbled and dropped the cash. Nixon would have pocketed it.'

(To digress for a moment, it was Richard Nixon who delivered some famous political last words in November 1962 when he told the US press, 'But as I leave you I want you to know – just think how much you're going to be missing. You won't have Nixon to kick around any more because, gentlemen, this is my last press conference . . . ' How different American political life might have been if he had stuck to that. But running for and winning the Republican nomination in 1968 changed all that.)

Among members of the British Labour party, opinions about Ronald Reagan have seldom been charitable. During the build up to the Falklands War the British Government had asked the US President to warn General Galtieri that an invasion was a *casus belli*. During the debate on the Franks Report which examined the causes of the war, Denis Healey was allowed to comment that *casus belli* was 'a phrase not safe to entrust to President Reagan'.

In Conservative ranks, support for Ronald Reagan was by no means assured. On the night of the 1980 presidential election Norman Tebbit was asked at a party at the US embassy if he was rooting for the Republicans. 'I'm a George Bush man myself,' he answered. 'I support the double ticket: Reagan and a heart attack.' Not many of Mrs Thatcher's colleagues, one suspects, would so openly have stepped out of line. Those who did were left in no doubt of the consequences.

One of these unfortunates was Jonathan Aitken. At the time of the 1975 Tory leadership contest he was on a business trip to Saudi Arabia and while there was interviewed by a local English language newspaper. The paper was interested in the candidates standing for leader of the Conservative party. What were their views on the Middle

East? Mr Aitken was happy to share his thoughts which included the comment on Margaret Thatcher, 'I wouldn't say she was open minded on the Middle East so much as empty headed. For instance, she probably thinks that Sinai is the plural of sinus.'

Had *Private Eye* not come across the interview and printed it after Mrs Thatcher's election that would have been the end of the matter. As it turned out, the lady did protest (whether too much or not, is not for me to say) and Jonathan Aitken found himself confronted by an uncompromising Airey Neave. Mrs Thatcher wanted to know if what *Private Eye* had printed was true; if it was, she wanted an apology.

Aitken said that it was, though his remarks weren't meant to be taken seriously. 'I'll drop her a line,' he concluded.

'That will not do,' Neave told him. 'She requires you to apologize in person.'

'Of course,' answered Aitken, 'I'll have a word next time I bump into her.'

'Nor will that do. She has asked me to tell you that she will see you in the Lobby tonight, after the Division at 10.15. She will be wearing green.'

Lord Soames was one of Mrs Thatcher's ministers who refused to conform to the convention of ministerial resignation whereby sacker and sacked write agreeable farewells to each other and go their separate ways with scarcely a mention of the cause of their parting. Lord Soames was Leader of the Lords until he got the shove and he was not so happy about his dismissal. 'Dear Margaret,' he wrote. 'You have asked me to resign. This I hereby do. Yours, Christopher.'

Norman St John-Stevas (as he then was) could usually be relied on to offer some modest resistance to his leader when the opportunity arose. As one of the more note-worthy dressers at Westminster he left a Shadow Cabinet meeting shortly before the 1979 general election, explaining that he had to attend a function.

'But Norman,' reprimanded his leader, 'I'm going there as well, and I'm not leaving the meeting.'

'Ah, but Margaret,' he told her, 'it takes me so much longer to change than you.'

(On the subject of prime ministerial couture, this recalls the splendid encounter that took place at one of Mrs Thatcher's regular audiences with the Queen, not long after the Conservatives' first election victory under her leadership. To the Prime Minister's dismay she arrived at the palace to find Her Majesty wearing an identical outfit. Come the following week an aide at Number 10 rang ahead to enquire how the Queen would be dressed when they next met. 'There's no need to worry,' came the reply from the Royal Household. 'Her Majesty never takes any notice of what her visitors are wearing.')

In Dame Rebecca West's opinion, 'Margaret Thatcher has one great advantage . . . she is a daughter of the people and looks trim . . . Shirley Williams has such an advantage over her because she's a member of the upper middle class and can achieve the kitchen-sink-revolutionary look that one cannot get unless one has been to a really good school.' (This has an echo of Bertrand Russell's dismissal of Anthony Eden, 'Not a gentleman; dresses too well.')

With only a few exceptions male MPs are generally castigated for their turn-out; at least they were before television cameras invaded the debating chamber. One Labour member who used to take it upon himself to challenge any breach of parliamentary procedure with the unnerving opening line, 'I don't think we've been introduced', was brought up short by a timely retort from an executive from the loftiest heights of BBC management. 'Oh yes, we have,' said the man from Auntie, 'about thirteen years ago. I think you were wearing the same suit.'

Sir Nicholas Fairbairn was one of the rare band of male MPs who manifestly paid some attention to his appearance. As Solicitor-General for Scotland he was entitled to wear a full-bottomed wig. This was a right he exercised with enthusiasm, drawing the comment from a junior lawyer present at a trial in which he was appearing, 'I thought I had wandered on to the set of a particularly bad amateur production of *Iolanthe.*'

Fairbairn succeeded Sir Alec Douglas-Home in the seat of Kinross and West Perth. In the course of offering his support to the would-be incumbent Sir Alec visited the constituency with a senior official from the local Conservative party. After a couple of days in the company of the former Prime Minister the local Tory was moved to comment on the contrast between him and his successor, who cut a very different figure as he went about his canvassing. This provoked some silent debate in Sir Alec's mind before he replied, 'Yes, I did hear that he campaigned in Crieff wearing lilac gloves.'

When Keir Hardie arrived at the House of Commons on his first day as an MP, the policeman on duty stopped the ex-miner dressed in his working clothes and cloth cap and asked, 'Are you working here?'

'Yes,' Hardie replied.

'On the roof?'

'No – on the floor,' said the new member for West Ham South.

Perhaps there is something to be said for MPs who dress distinctively. If nothing else they avoid the humiliation of mistaken identity. Not long after the Labour Party moved to its headquarters in Walworth Road, Michael

Foot, as party leader, was detailed to greet a band of fund-raising marchers who had been walking all the way from the Dorset village of Tolpuddle (whence the eponymous martyrs were transported in 1834). A crowd had gathered to salute this noble gesture in the cause of Socialism and in the spirit of the hour a small boy ran forward and eagerly shook Foot's hand. The Labour Party leader responded warmly. The boy then rushed back to his mother exclaiming: 'That's really made my day, Mum! Just think, I've shaken hands with Tony Benn!'

During his time as shadow to Michael Heseltine, Roy Hattersley was interviewed on a regional radio station, to comment on a recent decision by his opposite number. The interviewer, a nervous young man, began by asking, 'Er, I wonder if I could ask you, Mr Heseltine . . .'

'The name is Hattersley,' he was corrected. 'I'm the natural blond.'

One night in the early years of this century, three diners emerged from the Beefsteak Club having enjoyed an exceedingly convivial evening which had left them none too steady on their feet. In this state they attracted the attention of a patrolling policeman who asked them to identify themselves. One said that he was the Belgian envoy. Another gave his name as the Speaker of the House of Commons.

'And I suppose that you're the Prime Minister of England?' enquired the officer of the third.

'Yes, as a matter of fact I am,' answered Lord Balfour. He didn't fare much better on a visit to Scotland. At a dinner given in his honour, Balfour became aware of his host's young daughter eyeing him intently. He smiled at her, which encouraged her to ask, 'Are you really and truly an English lord?'

'Yes – really and truly,' he answered.

'I have often thought I should like to see an English lord,' she continued, 'and . . . and . . . '

'And now are you satisfied?'

'N-no,' she replied, 'I am not satisfied; I am a good deal disappointed.'

Perhaps she would have been better pleased by the Scottish credentials of Lord Home, who always managed to find the right thing to say in the least promising circumstances. Recognized on a train journey between Edinburgh and London he was greeted effusively by a middle-aged woman travelling with her husband.

'Ooh, it's Sir Alec Douglas-Home, isn't it?' she said. 'How marvellous to see you. I've always admired you and I tell my husband that the greatest tragedy of British life is that you never became Prime Minister!'

'Thank you so very much,' Sir Alec replied graciously. 'As a matter of fact I was Prime Minister – but only for a very short time.'

When William Waldegrave was first made a minister, his wife was in the gallery to listen to one of his early speeches. Next to her was an agreeable if otherwise unremarkable, middle-aged woman who noticed her obvious anxiety and said comfortingly, 'You look very nervous, my dear.'

'Yes I am,' the minister's wife answered. 'You see that's my husband down there.'

'Ah yes,' said the elder woman soothingly, 'I do know what it's like. You see my husband was Prime Minister for quite a few years, and I'm afraid you'll find it gets worse.' She was Mary Wilson and she knew what she was talking about. But as her husband was wont to comment, 'A week is a long time in politics.'

It is in journalism too if this experience of the Irish politician Garret FitzGerald is anything to go by. Once

upon a time he had been Dublin correspondent for the
Financial Times – but it really had been a long, long time
ago and his career had made him the subject of press
copy rather than its author. However, the *FT* needed a
piece in a hurry and with its staff correspondent unavail-
able the search was on for an old hack to pull together
the article in double-quick time. Somehow or other
Fitzgerald's telephone number was turned up and a call
went out that five hundred words were needed by nine
that evening.

'But you don't understand,' replied FitzGerald. 'I'm the
Foreign Minister now.' To his credit he didn't let this pre-
vent him from filing the piece as requested.

Leaving public office is harder. Churchill knew about
this. Following his second stroke he tottered painfully
into the chamber with the aid of a couple of sticks. 'The
old man's very ga-ga,' said one young Tory to another.
'He's also very hard of hearing,' growled Churchill as he
hobbled by.

Not long before his death he gave an interview to a
young reporter. When the time came to leave the young
man expressed his thanks and asked, 'I wonder if I might
be able to interview you again next year?'

'I see no reason why you shouldn't,' replied Churchill.
'You appear to be a healthy enough young man, and will
probably survive till then.' (Sir Malcolm Sargent came up
with more or less the same answer when he was asked to
what he attributed his advanced age of seventy and
replied, 'I suppose I must attribute it to the fact that I
haven't died yet.')

For former US President Calvin Coolidge, life after the
White House held little promise. In retirement he was
visited by a reporter who commented on the cars passing
his house, 'It must make you proud to see all these peo-

ple coming by here, merely to look at you sitting on the porch. It shows that although you are an ex-President you are not forgotten. Just look at the number of those cars.'

'Not as many as yesterday,' Coolidge answered. 'There were 163 then.'

By Coolidge's standards that was a lengthy conversation. 'I think the American people want a solemn ass as a President,' he once told Ethel Barrymore. 'And I think I'll go along with that.'

When Coolidge became vice president his successor as governor of Massachusetts visited him in Washington. One aspect of Coolidge's term as governor impressed him particularly. In spite of receiving a great many callers each day, Coolidge was always able to leave his desk by five in the afternoon. By contrast his successor was regularly in his office until nine in the evening. 'How come the difference?' he wanted to know.

'You talk back,' said Coolidge.

At a Washington dinner the woman seated beside him said, 'You must talk to me, Mr Coolidge, I made a bet today that I could get more than two words out of you.'

'You lose,' said the vice president, poker-faced.

The humorist Will Rogers had better luck. A friend bet him that he wouldn't be able to make Coolidge laugh inside two minutes. Rogers said he would do it in twenty seconds.

The two men were introduced.

'Mr President, this is Mr Will Rogers; Mr Rogers, President Coolidge.'

Rogers held out his hand, then a look of embarrassment clouded his face. 'Er, excuse me. I didn't quite get the name.'

Coolidge's grin won him the bet.

Summing up Coolidge's term in office, H L Mencken concluded, 'There were no thrills while he reigned, but neither were there any headaches. He had no ideas but he was not a nuisance.'

Chauncey Depew on the other hand was a politician who enjoyed the sound of his own voice and who once commented, 'On 23 April Shakespeare, St George and myself were born, and I am the only survivor.' Depew was a large man in every sense. So was William Howard Taft. At a dinner before Taft became president, Depew said of his equally obese 'colleague', 'I hope, if it is a girl, Mr Taft will name it for his charming wife.'

'If it is a girl,' replied Taft, 'I shall, of course, name it for my lovely helpmate of many years. And if it is a boy, I shall claim the father's prerogative and name it Junior. But, if as I suspect, it is only a bag of wind, I shall name it Chauncey Depew.'

Churchill and Attlee once indulged in a similar exchange in a gentlemen's lavatory in the House of Commons. Churchill entered, found Attlee already at the urinal and took up position at the other end.

'Feeling standoffish today, are we, Winston?' asked Attlee.

'That's right,' replied Churchill. 'Every time you see something big, you want to nationalize it.'

'At least you'll have to admit that he's very modest,' a colleague said to Churchill of Attlee.

'Absolutely true,' agreed Churchill, 'but then he does have a lot to be modest about.'

Attlee's restrained manner may have lacked Churchill's passion, but politically it served him well. Presiding over a meeting of the Parliamentary Labour Party soon after the end of the war the subject of the atom bomb, at that time still a fresh and awesome topic, appeared on the agenda. Harold Davies waxed lyrical in a forceful and emotive speech which brought cheers of approval from his fellows when he finished. Attlee listened impassively until the adulation had died away and then remarked crisply, 'Yes, Harold, that is something we'll have to watch. Next business.'

As the architect of post-war austerity, Sir Stafford Cripps, Attlee's Chancellor of the Exchequer after Hugh Dalton had resigned from the post, succeeded in asserting a moral and intellectual superiority which Churchill for one found hard to swallow. 'The trouble is, his chest is a cage in which two squirrels are at war,' commented Churchill, 'his conscience and his career.' Better known is his quip on Cripps as Chancellor, 'There but for the grace of God, goes God.'

Of Ramsay MacDonald, whom he once referred to as ' . . . the boneless wonder', Churchill said in a Commons speech, 'We know that he has, more than any other man, the gift of compressing the largest amount of words into the smallest amount of thought.'

Whereas Churchill took great delight in achieving the opposite. Asked by a reporter for his opinion of New York, the moment he stepped ashore from a visit, Churchill gave him what he wanted in seven words, 'Newspapers too thick, lavatory paper too thin.'

Discussing an MP recently arrived at Westminster, Churchill was intrigued by the man's name. 'Bossom? Bossom? What an extraordinary name,' he reflected. 'Neither one thing nor the other.'

None who deserved it were spared the Churchillian put down. Sir William Joynson-Hicks, a fellow Tory who held a number of ministerial posts during the 1920s, was addressing the Commons one day when he spotted Churchill vigorously shaking his head.

'I see that my right honourable friend is shaking his head,' said the minister. 'I wish to remind him that I am only expressing my own opinion.'

'And I wish to remind the speaker that I am only shaking my own head,' retorted Churchill.

During the war he had cause to rebuke one of his generals who had expressed the opinion that 'putting the troops in the picture was the sort of familiarity that breeds contempt'.

'You know, general,' replied Churchill, 'without a certain amount of familiarity it is extraordinarily difficult to breed anything at all.'

When the occasion demanded, though, his words and mien reflected quite different qualities of leadership. Again during the war he summoned a New Zealand airman to 10 Downing Street, to hear at first hand about the act of incredible courage that had recently won him a Victoria Cross. Shy and tongue-tied in the great man's presence, Sergeant Ward displayed none of the cool nerve that had enabled him to clamber onto the wing of his burning bomber 13,000 feet above the Zuider Zee, with only a rope round his waist, to put out an engine fire, and then inch his way back to safety inside the aircraft.

Churchill asked a few questions and receiving no answer, said to him gently, 'You must feel very humble and awkward in my presence.'

'Yes, sir,' Ward was able to answer.

'Then you can imagine how humble and awkward I feel in yours?' said the Prime Minister.

Lloyd George for one appreciated the secret of Churchill's success when he noted, 'Winston was nervous before a speech, but he was not shy . . . Winston would go up to his Creator and say that he would very much like to meet His Son, about whom he had heard a great deal and, if possible, would like to call on the Holy Ghost. Winston *loved* meeting people.'

Lloyd George also knew how to make the most from new acquaintances. The chairman of a meeting he was about to address gave these words of introduction, 'I had expected to find Mr Lloyd George a big man in every sense. But you see for yourselves he is quite small in stature.'

'In North Wales,' replied the guest speaker, 'we measure a man from his chin up. You evidently measure him from his chin down' – a quip which reminds me of one of Harold Macmillan's best remarks on Harold Wilson. Hearing that his Labour opposite number had been packed off to school without boots, Macmillan responded, 'That was probably because his boots were too big for him.'

The same laconic manner held him in good stead when he and Khrushchev had their celebrated clash at the UN in 1960. Macmillan was in the middle of a speech when the Soviet leader, who had taken off a shoe, began banging it on the table. The atmosphere was electric, but Macmillan only paused to remark, 'I'd like that translated, if I may.'

Before his fall from power in 1964 Khrushchev was addressing a large Soviet audience on the evils of the Stalin years. It was a long speech received in almost total silence until a voice was heard from the back of the hall, demanding, 'Why didn't you restrain Stalin? You were one of his colleagues?'

A leaden silence descended. There was not a murmur or a movement. Khrushchev's gaze ran over the rows of delegates before he thundered, 'Who said that?'

Still no one moved. The tension mounted unbearably

until Khrushchev said quietly, 'Now you know why.'

Closer to home Aneurin Bevan provoked similar disdain in Macmillan as Khrushchev. During a pre-war debate in the Commons Macmillan said of Bevan, 'He enjoys prophesying the imminent fall of the capitalist system, and is prepared to play a part, any part, in its burial, except that of mute.'

Bevan could trade insults with the best of opponents – and frequently with great style. Neville Chamberlain was often in his sights. When Chamberlain was Minister of Health in 1929, Bevan told Parliament, 'The worst thing I can say about democracy is that it has tolerated the right honourable gentleman for four and a half years.'

Eight years later he wrote in the *Tribune*, 'Listening to a speech by Chamberlain is like paying a visit to Woolworths; everything in its place and nothing above sixpence.'

From Lloyd George's point of view Chamberlain, 'saw foreign policy through the wrong end of a municipal drainpipe.'

Chamberlain's father, Joseph, seemed able to eschew his son's world-weary preoccupation. Indeed until well into old age he appeared remarkably spry, which he attributed to an interesting formula, 'Never walk if you can drive; and of two cigars always choose the longest and the strongest.'

When he resigned from Gladstone's government over the latter's Home Rule Bill, Chamberlain senior was not alone among fellow Liberals who found their leader hard to endure. 'I don't object to Gladstone always having the ace of trumps up his sleeve,' said Henry Labouchere, 'but merely his belief that the Almighty put it there.'

Queen Victoria didn't care for Gladstone's manner, 'He speaks to me as if I was a public meeting.'

And Disraeli, asked to distinguish between a misfortune and a calamity, offered the definition, 'If Mr Gladstone fell into the Thames, it would be a misfortune: but, if someone pulled him out, it would be a calamity.' Although he also said of his rival, 'He has not a single redeeming defect.'

During one of their frequent Parliamentary clashes Gladstone shouted the accusation, 'Mr Disraeli cannot possibly be sure of his facts.'

Disraeli responded, 'I wish I could be as sure of anything as my opponent is of everything.'

When the Irish Roman Catholic leader, Daniel O'Connell, cited Disraeli's Jewish ancestry in one tirade against him, Disraeli's reply carried dignity and weight. 'Yes, I am a Jew,' he answered, 'and when the ancestors of the right honourable gentleman were brutal savages in an unknown island, mine were priests in the temple of Solomon.'

(Mahatma Gandhi would have agreed with him here. When an interviewer asked him what he thought of western civilization he answered, 'I think it would be a very good idea.')

Turning the tables on an opponent was one of Disraeli's most polished parliamentary accomplishments. In a wonderful parody of Gladstonian oratory, he once described his opponent as, 'A sophisticated rhetorician, inebriated with the exuberance of his own verbosity, and gifted with an egotistical imagination that can at all times command an interminable and inconsistent series of arguments, malign an opponent and glorify himself.'

The late George Brown fell into this trap, as he was inclined to fall into other unforeseen hazards (by his own admission 'Most British statesmen have either drunk too much or womanized too much. I never fell

into the second category'). After commenting sourly that
the Labour Party under Michael Foot was being led by
someone with one eye and one leg, a colleague of the
Labour leader's remarked, 'Well, in the country of the
legless the one-eyed man is king.'

Rab Butler, George Brown's contemporary from the
Tory benches, was a past master of the well-honed snub.
At the Carlton Club lunching one day, Butler and a fellow Tory enjoyed a friendly conversation until the time
came for the MP to leave and bid Butler farewell. As he
was walking out of the dining-room he overheard Butler
being asked, 'Who was that?' which was followed by the
reply, spoken just loud enough to ensure he was in
earshot, 'Oh, that's X. He's of no significance.'

The story is told at Westminster of a senior Tory politician, cast in the mould of Rab Butler, who greeted a new
member fulsomely after the latter's maiden speech with,
'My dear fellow, that was a Rolls-Royce of a speech!'

Deeply gratified the new member was quick to pass on
this praise. 'He says that to all the new members,' a friend
confided. 'What he meant was that you were well oiled,
almost inaudible and carried on for a very, very long
time.'

Butler had the same happy ability to be withering even
when he was ostensibly complimentary. Running
through the agenda for the Conservative party conference, as he did with political correspondents year after
year, he would come to his Prime Minister's offering and
say, 'And then of course dear Anthony will make the
speech he always makes so well.'

Tony Benn is another political Anthony with a penchant
for banging the same drum. Cut short by Jim Callaghan
during one of his interminable diatribes in Cabinet, Benn
answered, 'I plead guilty, Prime Minister, and I ask for

ninety other offences to be taken into consideration.'

Some forty years earlier Aneurin Bevan expressed grudging bewilderment at the way Stanley Baldwin was able to baffle and seduce even his opponents in parliamentary debates. 'It is medicine man talk,' he wrote in the *Tribune* in 1937. 'It lifts the discussion on to so abstract a plane that the minds of the hearers are relieved of the effort of considering the details of the immediate problems. It imposes no intellectual strain because thought drifts into thought, assembling and dissolving like clouds in the upper air, having no connection with earthly obstacles. It flatters, because it appears to offer intimate companionship with a rare and noble spirit. It pleases the unsceptical, because it blurs the outline of unpleasant fact in a maze of meaningless generalities. Over and over again I have been amazed by the ease with which even Labour members are deceived by this nonsense. Murmurs of admiration break out as this second-rate orator trails his tawdry wisps of mist over the parliamentary scene.'

When there were pre-election proposals to replace Baldwin as party leader, F E Smith (then Lord Birkenhead) commented, 'I see no point in swapping donkeys when crossing a stream.' And when Baldwin retired, Winston Churchill commented, '. . . Not dead. But the candle in that great turnip has gone out.'

Of course Baldwin was something of an unexpected premier when he succeeded Bonar Law. Not that Bonar Law was exactly a firebrand at Number 10. When his ashes were interred in Westminster Abbey, H H Asquith spoke for many when he noted, 'It is fitting that we should have buried the Unknown Prime Minister by the side of the Unknown Soldier.'

Lloyd George recalled that Bonar Law was not an easy

companion even away from the Commons. The two of them were travelling together in France and Lloyd George recorded one particularly trying conversation, 'I told Bonar that . . . I had been to a Mozart concert and the music was wonderful. Bonar casually and languidly remarked, "I don't care for music." As we motored along, there was the Mediterranean blue sea on one side and the rolling snow-capped Alpes Maritimes on the other. This inspired me to exclaim, "Look, Bonar, what a wonderful scene that is."

'"I don't care for scenery," remarked Bonar.

'Presently we came to a bridge from which a group of local ladies could be seen bathing . . . I said to Bonar, "Look, Bonar, aren't those handsome women?"

'"I don't care for women," remarked Bonar very dryly.

'"Then what the hell do you care for?" I asked.

'Then in his very soft voice, and quieter still, Bonar replied, "I like bridge."'

Lord Curzon had every expectation of becoming Prime Minister after Bonar Law and Baldwin's appointment was a bitter blow. As Baldwin remarked, 'I met Curzon in Downing Street, from whom I got the sort of greeting a corpse would give to an undertaker.'

Max Beerbohm dismissed Curzon as Britannia's butler and even in his undergraduate days his stiff, unbending self-importance was the butt of university humour. As one rhyme put it:

My name is George Nathaniel Curzon,
I am a most superior person,
My cheek is pink, my hair is sleek,
I dine at Blenheim once a week.

In later life Curzon served as Vice-Chancellor of

Oxford and, when Queen Mary was awarded an honorary degree there in 1922, Curzon was asked in advance to approve the menu for the lunch at which she was to be entertained. This he returned to the bursar of Balliol with the sole comment, 'Gentlemen do not take soup at luncheon.'

One gets the impression that Queen Mary would have been more than up to passing similar censure herself. Dame Laura Knight, the distinguished English painter, told the story of one encounter she had at the Royal Academy. Her Majesty was in the habit of requesting a very private 'Private View' the night before the Royal Academy dinner, when she and her lady-in-waiting would walk in solitary splendour around the whole exhibition. During these visits she liked as many artists as possible to be present and to stand by their paintings. On this occasion Dame Laura was in position next to her work and her husband, Harold, was a little further along the gallery next to his paintings. Coming first to Dame Laura's pictures, Queen Mary paused and chatted for several minutes, then moved on and addressed a few words to the next artist. But after looking at Harold Knight's paintings she continued on her way without comment. As she passed a little further along to talk to someone else, Harold shrugged his shoulders and said to his wife in a loud stage whisper, 'She doesn't like them.' Queen Mary turned mid-sentence and in an equally loud stage whisper shouted, 'She does!' before continuing her conversation.

Edward VII, Queen Mary's father-in-law, came in for equal shares of criticism from his family and the world at large. His father, Prince Albert, summed him up as having ' . . . remarkable social talent. He is lively, quick and sharp when his mind is set on anything, which is seldom . . . But usually his intellect is of no more use than a pistol packed in the bottom of a trunk if one were attacked in the robber-infested Apennines.' While in Lord Fisher's opinion, 'He wasn't clever, but he always did the right thing, which is better than brains.'

When Queen Mary gave birth to her first son, the future Edward VIII, a motion was laid before the House of Commons to congratulate Queen Victoria on the birth of her grandson. Keir Hardie spoke in the debate and his comments proved to be unnervingly prophetic 'last words' on the future monarch, 'From his childhood onward this boy will be surrounded by sycophants and flatterers by the score and will be taught to believe himself as of a superior creation. A line will be drawn between him and the people he is to be called upon some day to reign over. In due course, following the precedent which has already been set he will be sent on a tour round the world, and probably rumours of a morganatic alliance will follow and the end of it all will be the country will be called upon to foot the bill.'

When George V died, bringing Edward VIII to the throne, Princess Margaret, aged six at the time, commented, 'Grandpa is gone to heaven and I'm sure God is finding him very useful.'

It was a former Master of Magdalen, Edward VIII's college at Oxford, who adopted an equally matter-of-fact approach to the Almighty when it was announced that the son of the Mikado of Japan was to enter the college. An official from the Japanese embassy paid a visit to make the arrangements for the Crown Prince's arrival. The President, who was a stickler for protocol, asked how the new undergraduate should be addressed.

'At home it is customary to refer to him as the Son of God,' he was told hesitantly.

'That will present no problems,' replied the President,

'we are used to having the sons of distinguished men at Magdalen.'

Back in the 1920s the sovereign of another Asian country visited these shores and arrived at Victoria with much pomp and ceremony. The young Julian Amery (now MP) was among the crowd gathered to see the spectacle. Nearby a couple of Cockneys watched the splendidly attired monarch alight from the train before one asked who it was.

'That's the King of Arfgarnistan,' said his friend. This answer was only partially satisfactory because after a moment's pause the questioner asked, 'Who's king of the other arf, then?'

(This reminds me, if you'll forgive the digression, of a delightful confusion that befell the distinguished anthropologist and sailor, Thor Heyerdahl, on a visit to London. In a busy schedule of appointments he was booked to appear first on ITV and not long after on BBC television. To expedite this the BBC had arranged for a taxi to collect him from the ITV studio and whisk him to the Television Centre in time for his appearance on BBC. When Heyerdahl reached the lobby, however, there was no taxi-driver to meet him. After waiting a few minutes and becoming anxious about the time, he went up to a man in a flat cap who looked as if he might be a taxi-driver and who was obviously on the look-out for someone. 'I'm Thor Heyerdahl,' he said. 'Are you looking for me?'

'No mate,' the taxi-driver answered. 'They've sent me to pick up four Airedales for the BBC.')

Correct forms of address have long been a source of confusion and embarrassment – for those who aren't in the know. Archbishop Roberts was quick to correct one young interviewer who enquired hesitantly, 'Your Grace – or is it Father? I believe you prefer to be called Father?'

'Same as God, yes: Father,' said the Archbishop.

The day after he became US Secretary of State Henry Kissinger held a news conference at the end of which he was asked, 'Do you prefer being called "Mr Secretary" or "Dr Secretary"?'

'I don't stand on protocol,' answered Kissinger. 'If you will just call me "Excellency" it will be OK.'

American politicians frequently have a breezy way of dealing with subordinates. General George McClellan came in for a good deal of chiding by Lincoln who felt McClellan could have been more active as commander-in-chief of the Army of the Potomac during the Civil War. Lincoln once wrote,

> My dear McClellan,
> If you don't want to use the army, I should like to bor-
> row it for a while.
> Yours respectfully,
> A Lincoln.

Some time later Lincoln received a telegram from McClellan, 'Have captured two cows. What disposition should I make of them?'

'Milk 'em, George,' cabled back Lincoln.

In the case of Dwight D Eisenhower, the soldier and politician were combined with mixed results. For one commentator, David Halberstam, 'Golf had long symbolized the Eisenhower years – played by soft, boring men with ample waistlines who went around rich men's country-club courses in the company of wealthy businessmen and were tended by white-haired, dutiful Negroes.' But for Murray Kempton, writing two years before Eisenhower's death, 'He was the great tortoise upon whose back the world sat for eight years. We laughed at him; we talked wistfully about moving; and all the while we never knew the cunning beneath the shell.'

As far as Groucho Marx was concerned, 'I read a very interesting quote by Senator Kerr of Oklahoma. In summing up Ike, he said, "Eisenhower is the only living unknown soldier." Even this is giving him all the best of it.'

Monty played his part in post-war politics by sitting in the House of Lords and there his wartime bearing and sense of occasion served him well. Seated in the House one day listening to a debate, he turned to the man next to him and said calmly, 'Excuse me, but I'm having a coronary thrombosis' and then left the chamber in search of first aid, which confirmed that he had indeed had a heart attack.

Churchill had his detractors during the war, but Roosevelt had had to face the Depression as American President and his opponents were vociferous in their condemnation of his measures. One parody of Psalm 23, itself so often sung in memory of departed souls, listed some of the criticisms made of his administration:

Roosevelt is my shepherd, I am in want.
He maketh me to lie down on park benches;
He leadeth me beside the still factories.
He disturbeth my soul:
He leadeth me in the Paths of destruction for his
    Party's sake.
Yea, though I walk through the valley of recession,
I anticipate no recovery
For he is with me;
His promises and pipe dreams they no longer fool me.
He prepareth a reduction in my salary in the presence
    of my creditors;

He anointeth my small income with taxes;
Surely unemployment and poverty shall follow me all
      the days of the New Deal,
And I will dwell in a mortgaged house for ever.

As a parting note here are four terse lines in memory
of a type of politician many electors might recognize:

Here rests the body of our MP
Who promised lots for you and me.
His words his deeds did not fulfil
And though he's dead he's LYING STILL.

5

THE ENTERTAINER

Some people cannot bid farewell without telling us to behave well. So often 'Goodbye' becomes 'be good' and is expanded into several minutes of advice. Perhaps we are born with a drive to pass on those maxims we think will be most beneficial to society even when we are exchanging last words with people we hardly know. A son might expect a few words of wisdom from his father as he departs for foreign lands but unsolicited opinions are also directed at comparative strangers. What is it about those individuals who seem to be particular targets for precepts and preaching?

'Speak the speech, I pray you, as I pronounced it to you, trippingly on the tongue,' is the start of Hamlet's famous advice to the actors. There can be few professions which are offered more advice than is directed towards the one pursued by actors. It must be quite frustrating for these well meaning advisers to discover that many performers find it equally easy to give advice in return but find it difficult to accept.

The explanation is that when one works unsociable hours, in surroundings where the sun is shut out, in a career as unpredictable and hazardous as the theatre, then it is only too easy to contract the Jed Harris syndrome. The what, you may ask? Let me explain.

In the twenties there were four big successes on

Broadway within eighteen months – all of them produced by Jed Harris. But his run of luck did not end
there. Success piled on top of success. However, his confidence started to waver, and he suspected that he might
be ill and could even be going deaf. When Harris consulted a specialist he was relieved to find out that he could
hear the ticking of the doctor's gold watch. Even when
the consultant went to the far end of the room Harris
could still hear the watch. For the final part of the examination the doctor left the room and called back, 'Can you
hear it now?' Harris could. The doctor returned and sat
down, looking grave. He solemnly gave his diagnosis, 'Mr
Harris, there is nothing wrong with your hearing. You
just don't listen.'

An entire repertory company can contract the Jed
Harris syndrome. One such cast broke many a director's
heart until the management decided to bring in for the
last production of the season a martinet, prone to giving
copious notes to the assembled cast after each rehearsal.
An exhaustive set of notes preceded the final technical
run which turned out to be a disaster. Apprehensively the
cast assembled for a marathon notes session.

'After that fiasco, I have several pages of notes for you
all,' began the director, 'and I planned to give some
straight advice, but I can see how much advice is still left
from my last set of notes – unused.' With that he walked
off the stage and another technical rehearsal was called.

Of course it might just be possible that some directors
are less worth listening to than others. Dame Ellen Terry
believed so. When she had long established her reputation in classical roles, she appeared in a production
directed by a young man whose inexperience and lack of
flair was in inverse proportion to the opinion he held of
himself. Working with Dame Ellen on one scene, he pre-

scribed every piece of business, detailed every move and demonstrated most of the lines. Dame Ellen repeated all that he required to his satisfaction and then proposed, 'Now, if you don't mind, I'll just do that little extra something for which I am paid my enormous fee.'

Towards the end of the First World War Ellen Terry went to a school production of *Julius Caesar* where one of the cast, a ten-year-old by the name of Laurence Olivier, caught her eye. 'The boy who plays Brutus is already a great actor,' she commented after the performance. At the time Brutus did not appreciate the significance of such praise. Before the performance, when all the grown-ups were getting into a tizzy because the great actress was going to be out front, the young Olivier asked, 'Who is Ellen Terry?'

I remember Athene Seyler in a similar situation when another young director asked her blankly, 'What have you done?' Athene, who by then had been an actress for half a century, asked, 'Do you mean this morning?'

Then there was Frank Pettingell who was asked the same question and would not allow the young director to interrupt until he had enumerated every play he had done since 1910!

As a director Noël Coward could give more succinct advice. During rehearsals once he was having difficulty controlling his patience with a young actor who persisted in stopping the rehearsal to clarify his motive for each move and each line. With the rehearsal falling seriously behind schedule and yet another enquiry 'What is my motivation?' Coward finally snapped back, 'Your motivation is your pay packet on Friday. Now get on with it.'

When a drama student earnestly enquired of Spencer Tracy, 'What do you look for in a script?' Tracy answered without hesitation, 'Days off.'

It was Tracy too, not Coward, who is credited with offering brief, useful advice to a young hopeful, who was eager to discover the film star's secret. 'Learn your lines,' he was told, 'and don't bump into the furniture.'

In Garrick's day anyone could set themselves up as an actor if they felt so inclined, a situation which clearly generated considerable resentment, not to say frustration, in those who strived to elevate the status of their profession and of the art of drama itself. The following letter from Garrick to the Duchess of Portland is masterly in its polite but stinging dismissal of the wretched Mr Collins who for some inexplicable reason won her preferment. This is what Garrick wrote:

> Madam – I shall always be happy to obey yr Grace's commands, but our company at present is so full, and all the parts dispos'd of, that I could not without great injustice to those actors I have already engag'd, employ the person you recommended.
>
> I have given Mr Collins the best advice in my power, and apprais'd him that I shall be ready at the end of the season to examine his qualifications for the Stage – if your Grace will permit me to speak my mind, I think he has the most unpromising aspect for an actor I ever saw – a small pair of unmeaning eyes stuck in a round unthinking face are not the most desirable requisites for a hero, or a fine gentleman –
>
> I am madam
> Your Grace's most humble and devoted servant
>
> D Garrick

In becoming a successful actor there are other 'obstacles' that must be avoided. The actor and theatre manager, Sir Herbert Beerbohm Tree, was finding a scene with a novice actor difficult in rehearsal. The young man was told to move further back. When this didn't bring any improvement, Tree again stopped the scene and directed the supporting player to move still further back. Soon Tree felt it was necessary to stop once more and motion the young man yet further away. At this the worried young actor said, 'But if I go any further back I'll be right off the stage.'

'Exactly . . . ' came Tree's cool reply.

The message was similar and no doubt just as clear when J M Barrie offered words of direction to a tyro during the rehearsals of *Quality Street*. The young man was slowing down the rehearsal by seeking constant reassurance for every move and line. When he asked for direction from Barrie for the umpteenth time, his senior suggested, 'I should like you to convey when you are acting it that the man you portray has a brother in Shropshire who drinks port.'

Just as taxing would have been Jerome Kern's direction to a young actress with whom he had become more and more exasperated as she persisted with an affectation of speech which put considerable emphasis on rolling the letter 'r'. Kern's patience was exhausted when the actress asked, 'Tell me, Mr Kern, you want me to cr-r-ross the stage but I'm behind a table. How shall I get acr-r-ross?'

'Why, my dear, just r-r-roll over on your r's,' was his reply.

Irving had to curb youthful exuberance of a different form while rehearsing the opening scene of his 1882 production of *Romeo and Juliet*. A band of enthusiastic young actors had been cast as the retainers of the two rival families and they were eager to make an impression on the great man when the time came in the opening scene to set about each other with much brawling and sword-work and a good deal of violent realism. Irving watched the mêlée in silence until the prince and his followers entered. Then he stopped the fight and said, 'Very good, gentlemen very good. But don't fidget.'

For many years George Grossmith played leading parts in the Savoy operas, although his relationship with W S Gilbert was often acrimonious. During a rehearsal for *Iolanthe* Gilbert had been fussing over a detail of the blocking in one scene for far longer than was necessary, to the point where Grossmith complained to another member of the cast, 'We've been over this twenty times at least.'

'What's that I hear, Mr Grossmith?' asked Gilbert.

'Oh, I was just saying, Mr Gilbert, that I've rehearsed this confounded business until I feel a perfect fool.'

'Well, perhaps we can now talk on equal terms,' snapped Gilbert.

'I beg your pardon?' said Grossmith.

'I accept your apology,' replied Gilbert, with a smile.

Henrietta Hodson was another of Gilbert's company who found him difficult at times. In rehearsal one day she made a move expressly against Gilbert's directions, and went to sit on a chair centre stage. For some reason she missed the chair completely and landed heavily on the floor instead. 'Very good,' shouted Gilbert from the stalls, 'I always knew you would make an impression on the stage one day.'

Robert Atkins, whom we have already encountered, was a past master of ridicule at rehearsal. At the Open Air Theatre at Regent's Park he stopped a scene and bore down on a hopeless and helpless young actor with the awesome indictment, 'Scenery by God. The words by the greatest poet the world has ever known. A director – not bad, and then . . . *you* come on.'

At a read-through on the grass stage at Regent's Park a young actress failed to come in with her line. Atkins, noticing her sitting cross-legged and dejected, with her head in her lap, snapped at her, 'It's no good looking up your entrance, you've missed it.'

Mrs Patrick Campbell was a very different force to be reckoned with in rehearsal. On one occasion at the Abbey Theatre in Dublin, she let rip with a particularly violent tantrum which ended with her walking to the footlights and peering out into the auditorium where Yeats was pacing up and down in the stalls. 'I'd give anything to know what you're thinking,' shouted the lady.

'I'm thinking,' Yeats replied, 'of the master of a wayside Indian railway station who sent a message to his company's headquarters saying, "Tigress on the line: wire instructions."'

After Mrs Patrick Campbell had burst out at George Alexander during a performance of *The Masqueraders*, he sent his stage manager to her dressing-room with the message, 'Mr Alexander's compliments and will you please not laugh at him on stage?'

'My compliments to Mr Alexander,' she answered, 'and please tell him I never laugh at him until I get home.'

The American critic Heywood Broun exploited the last of the 'last word' to great effect in a legal tussle with the actor Geoffrey Steyne. 'Mr Steyne's performance was the worst to be seen in the contemporary theatre,' Broun wrote. Steyne took him to court over this and while the case was pending, Steyne appeared in another play which Heywood Broun also reviewed. His verdict this time read 'Mr Steyne's performance was not up to his usual standard.'

Having the last line is a big help when making an exit. In many classical plays, a good exit line is essential when leaving the stage.

Sir Ralph Richardson felt happier if he had the 'last word' as he exited. I had noticed this during rehearsals for *The Heiress* at the Theatre Royal, Haymarket. This was my first West End play and, as I did not have a large part, I was able to watch the way the skilled cast, which included Richardson and Peggy Ashcroft, shaped their performances. In his opening scene, Richardson had neither the line that brought him on stage nor the exit line. As his character, Dr Sloper, entered he was greeted by the maid, 'Good evening, Doctor' and he then had the line, 'Good evening, Maria.' From the second rehearsal onwards Richardson entered, looked surprised to see Maria and uttered, 'Ah!' That became the maid's cue. Similarly, the script had given the exit line to the maid with the sequence:

'Good night, Maria.'

'Good night, Doctor.'

As he left the stage, Richardson would react to Maria's farewell by stopping before he reached the door, then he would turn, look sorrowfully at her as though she could not be expected to know the emotional burden he was carrying, and exit after, 'Ahh . . . '

Death and decay were presented dramatically in a play which probably provided me with my most unusual exit lines. On a British Council tour of South America with Brenda Bruce we presented Samuel Beckett's *Happy Days*. Audiences found this difficult. The play is almost a monologue for a fifty-year-old woman who spends the first half of the play buried up to her waist in sand and for Act 2 is embedded up to her neck. I played the part of her husband, Willie, who is partly hidden in the sand. I heard that Beckett had regularly visited an aunt who had a wasting disease and had created in this play an image of decay. It doesn't sound much fun does it? In fact, at each performance I discovered something new in this complex work and many of the lines were funny. Like old soldiers these two characters do not die, they fade away. Winnie puts a brave face on her existence and I used to find the ending poignant. After she and Willie have failed to make physical contact, the dialogue runs:

> WINNIE   Have you gone off your head, Willie?
> (Pause.) Out of your poor old wits, Willie?
> Pause.
> WILLIE   (Just audible) Win.
> Pause. Winnie's eyes front. Happy expression appears, grows.
> WINNIE   Win! (Pause.) Oh this is a happy day!
> (Pause.) After all. (Pause.) So far.
> Pause. She hums tentatively beginning of song, then sings softly, musical-box tune . . .
> They look at each other. Long pause.
>   CURTAIN

Well, I warned you that it was an unusual play.

The control over the audience gained by the skilful delivery of an exit line is likely to be lost when filming. This was seen at the close of a famous scene in the film *Doctor in the House*. Dirk Bogarde, Donald Houston, Kenneth More and I played medical students and James Robertson Justice took the role of the irascible surgeon, Sir Lancelot Spratt. Gathered around a patient's bed, we were all meant to be benefiting from Sir Lancelot's technical explanation of the time needed for blood to clot. When the inattentive student was challenged by Sir

Lancelot's, 'You! What's the bleeding time?' Dirk Bogarde replied, 'Half past two, sir.' Whenever the film was shown this closing line gained such a laugh that several lines were lost at the start of the next scene.

Whenever I think of laughter on exit lines I recall the struggle I once had to keep a straight face after I had delivered the closing lines of the first half of a Shakespearean tragedy. During the Stratford-upon-Avon season of 1947 one of my roles was Aumerle in *Richard II*. At the point where the king has been deposed, the stage was left empty except for my character who remained standing on the steps looking down at the Bishop of Carlisle and Abbot of Westminster who had their backs to the audience. My final couplet was:

> You holy clergymen, is there no plot
> To rid the realm of this pernicious blot?

After a dramatic pause, the curtain would very slowly descend on that frozen picture. My two fellow actors had wagered that they could make me laugh on stage at that point. At each performance they would follow my rhyming couplet with their own, just loud enough for me, but not the audience, to hear:

> Wot?
> Apparently not!

They were creative in the varied ways they discovered to deliver those lines and I had constant practice in maintaining a freeze position under intense provocation.

Perhaps my task would have been easier if the scene had not always built up so much tension in the first place. This is the part of the play where King Richard II surrenders his kingdom to Bolingbroke who is later crowned as Henry IV. Richard's closing lines as king are very moving:

> Now mark me, how I will undo myself:
> I give this heavy weight from off my head
> And this unwieldy sceptre from my hand,
> The pride of kingly sway from out my heart
> With mine own tears I wash away my balm,
> With mine own hands I give away my crown,
> With mine own tongue deny my sacred state,
> With mine own breath release all duty's rites:
> All pomp and majesty I do forswear;
> My manors, rents, revenues I forgo:
> My acts, decrees, and statutes I deny:
> God pardon all oaths that are broke to me!
> God keep all vows unbroke that swear to thee!
> Make me, that nothing have, with nothing grieved,
> And thou with all pleased, that hast all achieved!
> Long mayst thou live in Richard's seat to sit,
> And soon lie Richard in an earthy pit!
> God save King Harry, unking'd Richard says,
> And send him many years of sunshine days!

That 1947 season at Stratford was memorable for me for another reason. I met an actress, Diana Mahony, one of whose parts was Helen in *Dr Faustus*. She was wonderful as she crossed the stage to the following lines spoken by Faustus:

> Was this the face that launched a thousand ships,
> And burnt the topless towers of Ilium?
> Sweet Helen, make me immortal with a kiss:
> Her lips suck forth my soul, see where it flies.
> Come, Helen, come, give me my soul again.

Here will I dwell, for heaven is in these lips.
And all is dross that is not Helena.

Reader, I married her.

So, I have always had a soft spot for the play. But some years later, in another production at Stratford, the director had decided that Helen should cross the stage naked. On Dr Faustus's line, 'Was this the face . . . ' Gillian Cadell, a great friend and wife of my agent John Cadell, leaned over and whispered wickedly, 'Dr Faustus must be the only man in the theatre looking at her *face.'*

Shelley Winters threw an interesting light on productions of this type. 'Nudity on stage? I think it's disgusting,' she commented. 'But if I were twenty-two with a great body, it would be artistic, tasteful, patriotic and a progressive religious experience.'

Bette Davis was predictably more trenchant in her opinion. Of Jayne Mansfield, whose bust measured well over forty inches, she said, 'Dramatic art in her opinion is knowing how to fill a sweater.'

Not that Miss Davis spared herself when the chips were down. When her career reached its low point she placed this advertisement in *Variety* and *The Hollywood Advertiser:*

Situation Wanted
Mother of three (10, 11 and 15). Divorcee. American. Thirty years' experience as an actress in motion pictures. Mobile still and more affable than rumour would have it. Wants steady employment in Hollywood. (Has had Broadway.) Bette Davis. References upon request.

And when she got wind of a rumour circulating in New York that she had died, her only comment was, 'With the newspaper strike on I wouldn't consider it.'

Greer Garson, Bette Davis's exact contemporary, neatly deflated a moment of glory for Joan Crawford. The year was 1945; the occasion the premiere of *Mildred Pierce*. As the final curtain fell the auditorium was filled with wild applause which Miss Crawford received enthusiastically. 'Well, none of us should be surprised,' whispered Miss Garson. 'After all, my dear, you are a tradition.'

Lilian Baylis, who most certainly was a tradition, deftly turned the tables on John Gielgud at the end of a successful season at the Old Vic. The young Gielgud, anxious to be taken seriously, told Miss Baylis that he would love to work with her again, but could not begin immediately because he had so many other engagements. 'That's right, dear,' she replied, 'you play all the young parts you can – while you're still able to.'

Josephine Hull would have sympathized. She it was who commented, 'Playing Shakespeare is very tiring. You never get to sit down unless you're a king.'

The subject of the dramatic art itself has provoked some memorable comments. A Hollywood film producer told the English actress, Sarah Douglas, how 'cruel and evil' she looked in *Superman II*, while off-screen she seemed to be such good fun, and asked her how she did it.

'In England, dear,' she answered, 'we call it acting.'

When Patricia Hayes was congratulated for her portrayal of Edna the Inebriated Woman on television, which was so convincing in spite of the fact that she didn't drink, her explanation was, 'It's the people who don't drink who know what those who do act like.'

Even Edith Evans was moved to make a disparaging remark, the only one I ever heard from her, when we were standing in the wings watching on stage an actress who had a substantial private income and for whom

Edith had little professional regard. Edith watched her and said quietly to me, 'It must be lovely to have her money and just play at it.'

My attempt to persuade Noël Coward to come to see me in *The Relapse* met with a very similar response.

'Nothing, my dear Donald . . . ' he began, beaming as only Noël Coward could beam. Surely I thought, that beginning must be followed by '. . . would give me greater pleasure'? Instead he continued '. . . would persuade me to see *The Relapse*.'

'Why ever not?'

'I saw Cyril Richard.'

Not to be outdone, I replied, 'I am very much better than he.'

'No doubt. He was abysmal.'

I can comfort myself in being in good company on this account at least. Sir Herbert Beerbohm Tree's *tour de force* as Hamlet was received by W S Gilbert with the simple comment that it was, 'Funny without being vulgar.'

Tree was frequently the butt of Irving's humour. When Irving had selected a horse for one of his productions he asked the owner about its previous experience on the stage. On one matter he was particularly anxious, 'Has it been trained for the stage?'

'Indeed, yes,' was the confident reply. 'In fact it recently supported Mr Tree in a play and gave every satisfaction, though I have to admit that now and again a passing flatulence did cause it to break wind.'

Irving smiled and said to the horse, 'Ah, a bit of a critic, eh?'

In some respects Tree invited barbed comments. 'It is difficult to live up to one's own posters . . . ' he admitted. 'When I pass my name in such large letters I blush, but at the same time I instinctively raise my hat.'

This was not a regard he extended to the rest of his company. William Armstrong, who as a twenty-year-old actor, worked in Tree's company told me of the occasion he tried to have his name moved from the very bottom on the poster. With some trepidation he approached his boss and asked him, 'Would you mind coming outside for a moment?'

Tree complied and outside the theatre, Armstrong pointed to the poster and said, 'You see, my name is at the very bottom . . . '

'Yes,' agreed Tree.

'Well, er . . . do you think it could possibly be . . . er . . . elevated . . . a little?'

Tree did not answer.

'Or if not,' Armstrong soldiered on, 'could it read, so and so, so and so, so and so, AND William Armstrong?'

Tree ruminated for a while. 'Ye-es – why not BUT.'

Gracie Allen was once offered $750 a week by Florenz Ziegfeld to appear in one of his London shows. That was fine she said, but what would the offer be if her husband and straight man, George Burns, was included in the deal?

'Five hundred,' answered Ziegfeld.

The worry of remaining in work has dogged actors down the centuries. When Dr Billy Graham met Edith Evans and flattered her by saying how much those with a religious calling could learn from actors in putting across their message, she responded, 'Ah, but you have the advantage over us. In the ministry you have long-term contracts.'

Tallulah Bankhead said, 'It is one of the tragic ironies of the theatre that only one man in it can count on steady work – the night watchman.'

If you will excuse another digression, let me tell of the

young actor in weekly rep who had a deep and barely disguised loathing for his leading man. He kept a diary and in it confided day by day all the details of his obsession. 'Tonight HE killed my exit round.' 'Tonight HE ruined my finest scene.' 'Tonight HE coughed on my best laugh line.'

Then came: 'Monday. 6.15 pm. Dear Diary. Tonight I think I am going to get the better of HIM. We open a new play and I have a speech fifteen minutes long. Downstage. In the light. Facing the audience – and HE is upstage, seated at a desk, with his back to the audience, writing a letter. I think I must win . . . '

A slightly drunken hand added, '11.45 pm *HE DRANK THE INK.'*

Perhaps a leaf out of the book of an enterprising young American actor might have been to his advantage. The actor in question had been trying for a part in Hollywood. His career has not really got off the ground after four years of pretty thankless toil and this film promised the break he had been waiting for. But it didn't work out. The producer took a liking to one of the others at the screen test and he got the part instead.

When the loser heard the news his disappointment knew no depth. Meanwhile the successful actor hopped on the first plane back to New York to spread the glad tidings. The loser knew his address. To it he sent a telegram reading, 'DISREGARD PREVIOUS WIRE', signed with the name of the film director.

Macready managed to arouse rancour among a good many of those who appeared with him, few more so than an unfortunate actor who played Claudius to Macready's Hamlet in a production which opened in Norwich. Throughout rehearsals Macready had consistently found fault with the poor man. On the opening night the worm turned and instead of dying upstage, as directed, Hamlet's stepfather dropped dead centre-stage on the very spot Macready had been reserving for his own demise.

'Die further upstage,' Macready hissed under his breath. 'What are you doing here? Get up and die elsewhere, sir.'

To his surprise, the recently deceased King of Denmark sat up and addressed the prince in a voice which was plainly audible throughout the house, 'Look here, Mr Macready, you've had your way at rehearsals; but I'm king now, and I shall die where I please.'

Although Hamlet presents a challenge to all actors, the role is so rich that most players can bring something worthwhile to its interpretation. Most players, but perhaps not all. Henry Irving had recently enjoyed critical acclaim in America for his portrayal of Hamlet when he heard that another actor, Wilson Barrett, intended to tour there with his production of the play. When Irving expressed some doubt oven the wisdom of this, Barrett indignantly remarked:

'You don't think you're the only actor who can play Hamlet, do you?'

'No,' replied Irving, 'but you are the only actor who can't.'

When Tom Mead was playing the Duke in Irving's 1879 production of *The Merchant of Venice*, he came to the great trial scene somewhat the worse for drink. 'Make room,' began Mead, 'and let him stand before our face. Shylock, the world thinks, and I think so too . . . ' but here he faltered.

'Go on, go on,' hissed Irving who was playing Shylock, but all thoughts of cruelty, the pound of flesh, brassy bosoms, even the Turks and Tartars had evaporated. Frantic, Tom Mead searched for a way out and went straight to his last line, 'We all expect a gentle answer, Jew.'

My friend Godfrey Tearle told me of an incident in a 1946 production of *Antony* and *Cleopatra*. He was playing Antony on the night that the actor taking the role of Eros fell ill. At the very last moment, a nervous, unrehearsed actor was sent on to help remove Antony's armour. The young stand-in did not prove manually dextrous and on hearing Antony's lines:

Unarm Eros; the long day's task is done,
And we must sleep. Off, pluck off;

he looked very shamefaced, said 'I'm so sorry,' and hastily left the stage.

Towards the end of his career John Barrymore's eccentricity and foul temper got the better of him. In 1939 he was fumbling through one of his last stage appearances when he dried completely. After gagging for a moment or two he managed to make his way to the wings and whisper, 'What's the next line? What's the line?'

'What's the play?' was the answer from the prompt corner. More endearing is the story of A E Matthews, towards the end of his long career. Mattie was making one of his last West End appearances, during the course of which he had to receive a crucial telephone call. One night the telephone rang on cue, Mattie picked up the receiver and promptly dried. This didn't throw him however, he merely proffered the receiver to the only other actor on stage and said, 'It's for you.'

Mattie's last memorable appearance was in 1953 in *The Manor of Northstead*. At eighty-four he was having considerable difficulty learning his part. 'I know you think I'm not going to know my lines,' he said to the director who was having difficulty hiding his mounting anxiety, 'but I promise you that even if we had to open next Monday I would be all right.'

'But Mattie we do open next Monday,' answered the director.

At the end of the last century the critic Clement Scott, wrote a telling review of a play which had been a disaster from start to finish. For one member of the company, however, he reserved this kindly mention, 'And the prompter, although heard at rare intervals soon became a favourite with the audience.'

Maybe Dorothy Parker had forebodings of similar notices when she sat glumly through the dress rehearsal of her play *Close Harmony*. At one point the director expressed his concern that the over-endowed leading lady should be wearing a bra. 'Good God, no,' replied Miss Parker. 'At least something in the play is moving.'

(I can't help remembering Sir Robert Helpmann's views on this when he arrived in Adelaide as director of the city's festival in which I was appearing with the Royal Shakespeare Company. Helpmann had just flown in from New York where he had seen the long-running nude review *Oh Calcutta!* At the airport he was asked whether nudity would soon be featuring in ballet.

'No,' answered Helpmann. 'There are certain parts of the male and female anatomy which keep swinging after the music stops.'

And, if I may add one further digression, there's Noël Coward's priceless summing up of David Storey's play *The Changing Room*, which as its title suggests included scenes where, shall we say, the cast changed their clothes. The play wasn't totally to Coward's liking, as he made clear when he left, 'I didn't pay three pounds fifty just to see half a dozen acorns and a chipolata.')

My friend Joyce Carey accompanied Coward to the

opening night of Leslie Howard's *Hamlet* in New York. As Howard delicately spoke the prince's opening line, 'A little more than kin and less than kind' Coward clutched Joyce's arm and whispered, 'Beautiful – beautiful.' Unfortunately the rest of Hamlet's 11,600-odd words were delivered with just the same delicacy, leaving the performance limp and impassive. In Howard's dressing-room afterwards, Coward embraced him saying, 'Oh Leslie, you know how I hate over-acting – and you could never over-act – but please, please try.'

The Master was seldom short of the right word. Commenting on the fairies' chorus in Rutland Boughton's *The Immortal Hour*, in which they chant the line, 'They laugh and are glad and are terrible,' Coward said, 'Yes, it's a perfect description of Ensa.'

Oscar Wilde, as one might expect, was able to contrive some memorable assessments of productions he found wanting. He was not too impressed by Irving's 1888 revival of *Macbeth*, in which Ellen Terry played Lady Macbeth. 'Judging from the banquet,' Wilde wrote, 'Lady Macbeth seems an economical housekeeper and evidently patronizes local industries for her husband's clothes and the servants' liveries, but she takes care to do her own shopping in Byzantium.'

After Sir Herbert Beerbohm Tree's success as Lord Illingworth in Wilde's play *A Woman of No Importance*, the author was amused to discover that his leading man began behaving like the character, adopting his mannerisms, and dropping *bon mots* just as he did on stage. 'Every day dear Herbert becomes *de plus en plus Oscarisé*,' said Wilde. 'It is a wonderful case of nature imitating art.'

Wilde's fellow playwright, George Bernard Shaw (here turned critic), wrote of *An Ideal Husband*, in the *Saturday Review*, 'Mr Wilde, an arch-artist, is so colossally lazy that he trifles even with the work by which an artist escapes work.'

Shaw summed up the career of the first knight of the stage, Sir Henry Irving, with the boldly dismissive statement, 'He achieved the feat of performing Hamlet with the part of Hamlet omitted and all other parts as well, substituting for it and for them the fascinating figure of Henry Irving, which for many years did not pall on his audience and never palled on himself.'

Writing again for the *Saturday Review*, Shaw reviewed another play (not by Oscar Wilde this time):

I am in a somewhat foolish position concerning a play at the Opéra Comique, whither I was bidden this day week. For some reason I was not supplied with a programme; so that I never learned the name of the play. At the end of the second act the play had advanced about as far as an ordinary dramatist would have brought it five minutes after the first rising of the curtain; or say, as far as Ibsen would have brought it ten years before that event. Taking advantage of the second interval to stroll out into the Strand for a little exercise, I unfortunately forgot all about my business, and actually reached home before it occurred to me that I had not seen the end of the play. Under these circumstances, it would ill become me to dogmatize on the merits of the work or its performance. I can only offer the management my apologies.

Shaw stands among a significant company of critics who have suffered equally bleak nights in the theatre. The New York critic Heywood Broun attended a Broadway opening night and afterwards filed the review, 'It opened at 8.40 sharp and closed at 10.40 dull.'

His fellow critic Robert Benchley could not stay the course when he was sent to review a play entitled *The Squall*. This was due in part to the dialogue which consisted largely of pidgin English. On hearing from a gypsy girl on stage, 'Me Nubi. Nubi good girl. Me stay,' Benchley took his cue, rose from his seat, announced, 'Me Bobby. Bobby bad boy. Me go,' and left the theatre.

George S Kaufman, friend of Broun and Benchley, produced many a well turned review himself. 'I saw the play at a disadvantage,' he wrote of one dull offering, 'the curtain was up'. 'There was laughter at the back of the theatre,' he commented on another, 'leading to the belief that someone was telling jokes back there.'

Kaufman dropped in to watch a performance of his play *Of Thee I Sing* and was horrified at the liberties the leading man, William Gaxton, was taking with the script. During the interval Kaufman dashed out of the theatre and sent Gaxton a telegram which read, 'Am sitting in the last row. Wish you were here.'

When Gertrude Lawrence appeared on Broadway in a straight play, Kaufman's verdict read, 'A bad play saved by a bad performance.'

Anthony Hope was not enthralled by *Peter Pan*. As he emerged from the opening night he commented, 'Oh, for an hour of Herod.'

Hope, the author of *Rupert of Henzau* and *The Prisoner of Zenda* would have felt more at home with Ivor Novello, though he was not everyone's cup of tea. In 1951 the *Evening Standard* carried the anonymous suggestion, 'It is time that some official recognition were shown of his achievement in keeping the British flag flying over Ruritania.'

James Agate knew something about musical comedy and regrettably for P G Wodehouse failed to find it when he went to the first night of *Oh Kay!* at His Majesty's Theatre in September 1927:

In so far as I can make anything of the imbroglio of this piece, it concerns a cretinous earl so harassed by the super tax, that he is reduced to rum-running in his last possession, his yacht. With him is his sister, who is apparently called Kay. Kay, clothed in a mackintosh, makes a burglarious midnight entry into the house of one Jimmy Winter, whom she had previously saved from drowning . . . Jimmy, who is arranging to marry a second wife before completely divorcing the first, now falls in love with Kay. It also happens that another rum-runner, 'Shorty' McGee, has also chosen Winter's house in which to store without permission his stock of illicit liquor. The establishment possesses forty unexplained housemaids and a baker's dozen of inexplicable footmen, who from time to time interrupt such action as there is. This is the entire story, and I can frankly say that I have known nothing in the musical comedy line of greater melancholy.

Not many people got the better of Agate, but Joyce Carey's mother, the actress Lillian Braithwaite, did when they met one day at the Ivy restaurant. The day in question carried a particular significance. Mrs Patrick Campbell had died that morning and Agate, detailed to write her obituary for the *Sunday Times*, and hurrying to meet the copy deadline, hoped a quick chat with Miss Braithwaite would provide him with the material he needed. So he approached her table with the greeting, 'My dear Lillian, I have always thought that you are the second best actress on the English stage,' fully expecting her to enquire who, in his opinion, was the best. Mrs

Patrick Campbell, he would answer and they would be off. However, his strategy was thwarted when she replied coolly, 'Thank you James, I appreciate that coming from our second best dramatic critic.'

Lillian Braithwaite could almost have been the subject of a book of last words herself. When she was appearing with Mary Jerrold in *Arsenic and Old Lace* it had been arranged that they should share the billing. On tour, however, this presented a problem and the company manager had to race ahead to the next theatre to change dressing-room 2 to dressing room A, so that one lady would have dressing-room 1 and the other dressing-room A. This worked well enough until the company arrived at the Grand Theatre, Leeds. Here the company manager found one enormous dressing-room which was virtually the size of a house when measured against the rabbit hutches that constituted the rest of the dressing-rooms. In Leeds there was no dressing-room 2 that could conceivably be disguised as dressing-room A.

On the Monday morning Lillian Braithwaite arrived at the theatre and immediately sent for the company manager to inform him that no dressing-room notice had been posted.

'I am sorry, Dame Lillian,' he apologized. 'I have a problem. No doubt you know that there is only one respectable dressing-room in this theatre.' Lillian knew that very well, which is why she had appeared.

'But, my dear, Miss Jerrold must have it,' she told the company manager. 'She was a leading lady when I was still at school.'

When Gilbert Harding met Mae West at a radio interview the atmosphere was also pretty cool. Miss West's manager was uncomfortable about Harding's interviewing technique and suggested that things might go better if he could sound a little sexier when talking to the star. Harding didn't take kindly to the idea, and answered, 'If, sir, I was endowed with the power of conveying unlimited sexual attraction through the potency of my voice, I would not be reduced to accepting a miserable pittance from the BBC for interviewing a faded female in a damp basement.'

Eric Maschwitz, the executive producer of my ITV series *Our Man at St Marks* told me a story which I greatly enjoyed about an out-of-town run. Before the war Eric had written lyrics for several popular songs as well as several musicals. One of these was *Good Night Vienna*, a poster for which he spotted outside the Lewisham Hippodrome when he was driving down to Kent one Friday evening. Eric couldn't resist popping into the theatre to enquire, 'And how is *Good Night Vienna* doing in Lewisham?'

'Just about as well as *Good Night Lewisham* would do in Vienna,' the manager informed him.

The success of any production is usually measured in part by the extent of the audience's approval and the box office returns. Oscar Wilde knew all about this. 'The play was a great success,' he said of one of that had failed to gain the level of popular response he had hoped for, 'but the audience was a disaster.'

Peter Bridge, the impresario to whom *Guilty Party* owed its success was fascinated by audiences. He had a questionnaire inserted in every programme during our run of the play, asking patrons all sorts of questions designed to tease from them their theatre-going habits. One evening Peter and I were leaving the theatre when some young girls stopped us to ask for my autograph. Never one to lose an opportunity, Peter presented his verbal questionnaire.

'Did you like the play?'

'Yes.'

'Why did you come to see this particular play?'

'Because we couldn't get seats for *The Mousetrap*.'

John Phillip Kemble, the great tragic actor, commanded the attention of an audience and expected to hold it. During a performance in a provincial theatre in 1820, it became evident that a young child in the audience was less enthralled with the performance and with Shakespeare's verse than might have been wished. Kemble battled on but the child's crying became more intrusive. At last Kemble stopped, came down to the footlights and proclaimed, 'Ladies and gentlemen, unless the play is stopped, the child cannot possibly continue,' and he strode off into the wings to sympathetic applause.

Ethel Barrymore had to do much the same once when she was appearing with Charles Cherry, an elderly character actor whose performances were only marginally impaired by his being a little deaf. They opened the play on stage together and were barely a minute or two into the first scene when a party of latecomers arrived noisily in one of the stage boxes and heedless of what was happening on stage continued to chatter as they settled themselves. Miss Barrymore allowed them to continue until they became so disruptive that she had to break off to say to them directly, 'Excuse me,' catching their attention at last. 'I can hear every word you are saying, but Mr Cherry is slightly hard of hearing. I wonder if you would speak up for him?'

Judi Dench was much praised for her performance in the Royal Shakespeare Company's production of Brecht's play *Mother Courage*. In one performance, however, disaster struck when a wheel fell off the wagon (the main prop) and the performance literally ground to a standstill.

The audience became restive and to explain the predicament Judi Dench walked downstage to announce, 'We can mend everything about this show except the wheels. Unfortunately we are the RSC, not the RAC.'

The noise of London trains thundering over Hungerford Bridge might reasonably have been expected to disrupt performances at the Playhouse Theatre. Dirk Bogarde put this very question to Gladys Cooper, who produced a disarmingly simple solution, 'Trains, dear? We had them stopped on matinée days, naturally.'

The very first night of *Arms and the Man* was generally well received and George Bernard Shaw was called on stage to take a bow. As he stepped forward to acknowledge the applause a lone voice could be heard shouting, 'Rubbish! Rubbish!'

'I quite agree with you,' answered Shaw genially, 'but who are we to argue against so many?'

Two years earlier Sarah Bernhardt had been playing Cleopatra to packed houses. Audiences particularly enjoyed her dying scene in which she systematically set about wrecking her palace with exuberant ferocity, before expiring among the debris. Night after night the house rose to its feet applauding wildly. At the end of one performance the commotion was dying away as one elderly woman in the stalls was overheard remarking to her companion, 'How different, how very different from the home life of our own dear queen.'

Seventy years after this Peter Dews directed *Antony and Cleopatra* at the Chichester Festival. One night he was in the foyer as the audience left after the performance when he overheard a woman remarking to her companion, 'Yes, and the funny thing is, exactly the same thing happened to Monica.'

There are occasions when the comments from the

house are less measured. When *Waiting for Godot* was first staged, cries of disapproval regularly punctuated performances. One night as Vladimir said to his companion, 'I am happy,' and Estragon replied, 'I am happy too,' a voice shouted out from the stalls, 'Well, I'm bloody well not.' When more restrained members of the audience tried to silence the protester, this only served only to egg him on. 'And nor are you. You've been hoaxed like me,' he insisted. This was followed by scuffles in the fifteen-and-sixpenny seats during which another member of the audience, the actor Hugh Burden, could be heard calling out: 'I think it's Godot.' His intervention caused sufficient amusement and diversion for the original source of the disturbance to be discreetly ejected from the theatre.

Henry James's play *Guy Domville* had a rough ride from its opening night. Produced by Sir George Alexander, who also took the title role, it was clear from the opening scenes that it was not going down well with the audience. As sometimes happens in cases like this, Sir George was faced with the infelicitous line, 'I am the last of the Domvilles,' which he had no sooner delivered than a voice shouted back from the gallery, 'Well, at any rate, that's a comfort to know.'

Fate does deal an even hand in these matters, however. Alfred Lunt and Lynn Fontanne were appearing together in London one night in 1944 when a V-2 rocket landed right outside the theatre. Miss Fontanne was on stage alone as the building shuddered with the force of the explosion and plaster cascaded from the walls and ceilings. Unfazed by this, Alfred Lunt entered on cue, supporting a piece of falling scenery on his way, and delivered his scripted line, 'Are you all right, darling?'

Surely the most poignant of any theatrical last words are those of Richard Brinsley Sheridan on the night that the Drury Lane Theatre burned to the ground. The splendid playhouse, the pride of the London stage, had been Sheridan's showpiece for thirty glorious but ruinous years. On the night of 24 February 1809 it was engulfed in an inferno which lit up the winter sky for miles around. Sheridan watched the blaze from the Piazza Coffee House in Covent Garden, where he had ordered a bottle of wine. The disaster he faced was plain to all but his remarkable composure drew words of admiration to which he replied, 'May not a man be allowed to drink a glass of wine by his own fireside?'

6

THE
DEAR
DEPARTED

As an actor, and this applies especially to those who play Shakespeare, one has the opportunity of rehearsing, refining and speaking some of the most perfectly phrased dying words ever written. It is fascinating therefore to discover what is actually said at the moment of death, or uttered unknowingly as a final word before the great reaper appears. For example, whenever I have been concerned onstage with an execution scene, I have found it difficult to forget the last words and end of the Duke of Monmouth. He was the natural son of King Charles II, who probably fathered at least another dozen illegitimate children by various mistresses. Monmouth had become one of Charles's favourites and on his father's death he claimed the throne and set up as rival to Charles's brother, James. His weak army was defeated and Monmouth was condemned as a traitor. At the block he met the executioner, Jack Ketch, who had not managed to dispatch his last victim quickly or cleanly. Apprehensively, Monmouth voiced his concern, 'Prithee, let me feel the axe. I feel it is not sharp enough.'

Monmouth's fears proved well founded. The executioner almost lost his nerve after three blows merely hacked poor Monmouth. One grisly report claims that Ketch finally had to cut through the neck with a knife.

Some dying words are banal, some full of pathos, some

witty to the end; some full of love; some full of malice; a few optimistic and full of good heart, a few naturally touched with dramatic irony. From Alexander the Great to Florenz Ziegfeld, here is a selection of my favourites:

Alexander the Great (356BC–232BC)
Managing to stay lucid in spite of his fever; Alexander replied to the question of who was to succeed him:
  'The strongest!'

Ethan Allen (1738–1789)
This officer of the American Revolutionary army was told that the angels were waiting for him:
  'Waiting are they, waiting are they? Well, let them wait!'

Phineas T Barnum (1819–1901)
A true showman to the end, he asked:
  'How were the receipts tonight at Madison Square Garden?'

Aubrey Beardsley (1872–1898)
The infamous artist of the *Yellow Books* said:
  'I am imploring you – burn all the indecent poems and drawings.'

Ludwig van Beethoven (1770–1827)
Stone deaf and suffering a long final illness his last words were:
  'I shall hear in heaven!'

Billy the Kid (1859–1881)
Approached by his killer, Sheriff Pat Garrett:
  'Who's there?'

Paulina Bonaparte (1780–1825)
Known for her vanity, Napoleon's sister said:
  'I always was beautiful.'

Lucretia Borgia (1480–1519)
With more to be forgiven than most women she wrote a final letter to the Pope:
  'I desire as a Christian, although I am a sinner, to ask your Holiness's blessing for my soul. Therefore I offer myself to you in all humility and commend my husband and my children, all of whom are your servants, to your Holiness's mercy.'

Andrew Bradford (d 1742)
The publisher of Philadelphia's first newspaper prayed:
  'O Lord, forgive the errata!'

John Brown (1800 –1859)
When his executioner asked him if he was tired, this anti-slavery campaigner replied:
  'No, but don't keep me waiting longer than necessary.'

Robert Browning (1812–1889)
On being told that his last volume of poems, *Asolando*, was well received:
  'How gratifying!'

Mme Jeanne Louise Henriette Campan (1752–1822)
Fast fading, she felt she had been too brisk in instructing a servant:
  'How imperious one is when one no longer has time to be polite.'

Charles II (1630–1685)
Of Nell Gwynn, his mistress and once rather a good comedy actress:

'Let not poor Nelly starve.'

Lord Chesterfield (1694–1773)
On greeting a visitor to his sick-room, the author of all those letters on correct behaviour said:

'Give Dayrolles a chair.'

Jean Baptiste Corot (1796–1875)
'I hope with all my heart there will be painting in heaven.'

Francis (Two Gun) Crowley (d 1931)
The bank robber and murderer said to those strapping him into the electric chair:

'You sons of bitches. Give my love to mother.'

John Philpot Curran (1750–1817)
The Irish writer and socialite, told by his doctor that he seemed to be coughing with more difficulty, answered:

'That's surprising, since I have been practising all night.'

Sir Everard Digby (d 1605)
The Gunpowder Plot conspirator gasped the most defiant of last words. As he was being hanged, drawn and quartered the executioner cried to the crowd, 'Behold the heart of a traitors,' to which Digby reputedly responded:

'Thou liest!'

Anthony J Drexell III (d 1893)
The American socialite proudly showed the fine trigger

on his loaded new pistol:

'Here's one you've never seen before . . .'

W C Fields (1879–1946)

Friends were surprised to discover Fields on his deathbed searching through the Bible. He explained:

'I'm looking for a loophole.'

Charles James Fox (1749–1806)

He was one of the few politicians satisfied enough with his achievements to claim:

'I die happy.'

Thomas Gainsborough (1727–1788)

With great optimism the artist claimed:

'We are all going to heaven, and Van Dyck is of the company.'

Johann Wolfgang von Goethe (1749–1832)

On his deathbed the great poet is attributed with the dying words:

'More light!'

Joseph Green (d 1863)

Checking his own pulse, this surgeon observed:

'Stopped.'

Neville Heath (d 1946)

As he was about to be hanged for murder he requested a whisky as a last wish and when he had almost drunk it, added:

'You might make that a double.'

Georg Wilhelm Hegel (1770–1831)
'Only one man ever understood me.'

Feeling the need as a philosopher to qualify this, he finally added, 'And he didn't understand me . . . '

Heinrich Heine (1797–1856)
When the German poet was asked the night before his death whether he was at peace, he answered:

'God will pardon me – it is His profession.'

A E Housman (1859–1936)
Housman also approached his end in a happy frame of mind. His doctor told him a joke about a judge who questioned the meaning of the description, 'a platinum blonde' asking, 'Am I to understand that as a precious metal or a common ore?'

Housman chuckled gently and replied:

'I'll tell that story on the golden floor.'

Henrik Ibsen (1828–1906)
When his wife suggested that he looked a little better, he answered:

'On the contrary.'

Sir Henry Arthur Jones (1851–1929)
When the playwright was asked if he would prefer his nurse or his niece to spend the night by his bedside, he replied:

'The prettier – now fight for it!'

(If Oscar Wilde is to be believed these are among the wittiest things Jones ever said; Wilde's tip on successful writing had been, 'The first rule for a young playwright to follow is not to write like Henry Arthur Jones . . . the second and third rules are the same.')

William Kidd (1645–1701)

Although he had been promised a pardon, the English pirate was brought to the gallows where he complained to his executioner:

'This is a very fickle and faithless generation.'

Charles Lamb (1775–1834)

On his deathbed he complained:

'My bedfellows are cramp and cough – we three all in one bed.'

St Lawrence (d 258)

When the Roman emperor Valerian was persecuting the Christians, Lawrence refused to hand over the Church's treasures but instead presented a crowd of the sick and the poor as the real treasures of the Church. For this he was sentenced to be roasted alive on a gridiron. St Augustine reported St Lawrence's last words as:

'I am roasted: turn me over and eat.'

Niccolo Machiavelli (1469–1530)

The Italian political theorist claimed:

'I desire to go to hell and not to heaven. In the former place I shall enjoy the company of popes, kings and princes, while in the latter are only beggars, monks and apostles.'

Marie Antoinette (1755–1793)

Approaching the guillotine, the Queen of France accidentally trod on the executioner's foot and said:

'Monsieur, I ask for pardon. I did not do it on purpose.'

Karl Marx (1818–1883)

When his housekeeper asked if he had any last message

for the world, he told her:

'Go on, get out! Last words are for fools who haven't said enough.'

W Somerset Maugham (1874–1965)
When he was asked for some final words of wisdom, the author offered these:

'Dying is a very dull, dreary affair. And my advice to you is to have nothing whatever to do with it.'

Baba Meher (d 1969)
Unusually, this guru uttered his last words forty-four years before he died. After taking a vow of silence in 1925, he finished speaking with the words:

'Don't worry, be happy,' and stayed silent for ever.

Elie Metchnikoff (1845–1916)
True to the end to his commitment to study and the advancement of human knowledge, the Russian bacteriologist finally gave the instructions to his research assistant:

'You remember your promise? You will do my post-mortem? And look at the intestines carefully, for I think there is something there now.'

Ramon Maria Narvaez (1800–1868)
When this Spanish statesman was asked by a priest if he had forgiven all his enemies, he replied:

'No need to forgive them – I have had them all shot.'

King Oscar II of Sweden (1829–1907)
In times of public emergency such as the outbreak of war, theatres are usually the first places to be closed. Happily, they are also the first places to be reopened. Oscar II had

it right when he gave his final instructions:

'Don't let them shut the theatres for me.'

John Palmer (1758–1798)

Much of John Palmer's acting career had been as a supporting actor in pot-boilers that never caught the public's imagination. His most celebrated theatrical success had to wait until the end of his life. He was appearing in a play entitled *The Stranger* and collapsed on stage and died as he spoke the line:

'There is another and a better world.'

Viscount Henry John Temple Palmerston (1784–1865)

Still capable of brave humour to the end, he said:

'Die, my dear doctor? That's the last thing I shall do.'

Carl Panzram (1891–1930)

Not content with, or repentant for, the murder of twenty-three people, he brazenly assured his executioner:

'I wish the whole human race had one neck and I had my hands around it.'

Charles W Peale (1741–1827)

Sensing he was near to the close of his long and eventful life, the American artist asked one of his daughters to take his pulse. She reported that she could feel nothing. Peale nodded and murmured:

'I thought not.'

Perugino (1445–1523)

As he lay dying this favourite artist of Pope Sixtus IV refused to make his final confession, saying to the priest:

'No. I am curious to see what happens in the next world to one who dies unshriven.'

Luigi Pirandello (1867–1936)

The Italian playwright's last requests were simple enough:

'The hearse, the horse, the driver, and – enough.'

William Pitt (the Younger) 1759–1806

The oral tradition reports the great politician's life ending with the remark:

'I think I could eat one of Bellamy's veal pies.'

Alexander Pushkin (1799–1837)

Dying from wounds sustained in a duel, the Russian writer was carried home and asked if there were friends he wished to see. He looked up at his bookshelves and said:

'Farewell, my friends.'

François Rabelais (1490–1553)

There was no sign of the coarse humour that coloured much of his writing when the creator of Gargantua said:

'Bring down the curtain: the farce is ended.'

James W Rodgers (1911–1960)

When this Utah murderer was brought before the firing-squad he was asked if he had any last requests and answered:

'Yes – a bulletproof vest.'

Meyer Amschel Rothschild (1743–1812)

The international financier instructed his five sons:

'Obey the law of Moses, remain united and always consult your mother. Observe these three points and you will soon be rich among the richest and the world will belong to you.'

Saki (1870–1916)

Saki was the pen-name of Hector Hugh Munro who served in the trenches in France. He would have known of the superstition that it was unlucky to light three cigarettes from the same match. The time this would have taken would have been long enough for an enemy sniper to take aim. Munro's last words were the understandable reproach:

'Put that bloody cigarette out!'

Samson (d 1155 BC)

Presumably it is the story of Samson that gives rise to the Green Room lament in a certain provincial theatre that even if you bring the house down there you still die the death. Generations of actors at that particular booking have gained some comfort from Samson's last words:

'Let me die with the Philistines.'

General John Sedgwick (1813–1864)

Fighting in the American Civil War, he observed:

'They couldn't hit an elephant at this dis . . . '

Adam Smith (1723–1845)

The political economist looked at the crowd of friends gathered to catch his last words of wisdom:

'I believe we must adjourn the meeting to some other place.'

Sydney Smith (1771–1845)

Told that he had probably drunk some ink by mistaken he ordered:

'Then bring me all the blotting paper in the house.'

Mrs Isidor Straus (d 1912)
As the *Titanic* sank, she declined to enter a lifeboat without her husband:
'We have been together for forty years and we will not separate now.'

Dylan Thomas (1914–1953)
His final claim was:
'I've had eighteen straight whiskies. I think that's the record . . . '

Voltaire (1694–1778)
A man not too fond of organized religions, Voltaire saw the bedside light flare and was heard to ask:
'The flames already?'

Oscar Wilde (1856–1900)
Calling for champagne:
'I am dying, as I have lived, beyond my means.'

Florenz Ziegfeld (1869–1932)
Ziegfeld imagined himself again at the first night of the 'Follies':
'Curtain! Fast music! Light! Ready for the last finale! Great!! The show looks good, the show looks good.'

Ziegfeld was one of the pallbearers at the funeral of Harry Houdini. As the great escapologist's coffin was lifted onto their shoulders, Charles Dillingham, another producer-cum-pallbearer, whispered, 'Do you think he's still inside?'

That story calls to mind the death of James Agate, or rather his memorial service. When he died in 1947 practically all London's theatrical memorial services were organized by George Bishop, theatre correspondent for the *Daily Telegraph*, and Charles La Trobe, stage director at the Haymarket Theatre. The stage-door keeper at the Haymarket in those days was a venerable and lovable old character called Bibby, whose only failing was his total inability to relay messages with any semblance of accuracy. So when Bishop telephoned La Trobe, and Bibby took the call, the message that reached La Trobe read, 'Mr A Gate will be at Sir Martin Field's at 11.30 and would like you to join him.'

Graveyards make suitable resting place for the quick as well as the dead. While I was making the BBC television series *Discovering English Churches* I used to spend the short breaks in filming to enjoy a prowl round churchyards. I was soon aware of the inscriptions left for us on tombstones by previous generations. It was often the old stones, so caked by lichens and weeds, that offered up the greatest treasures. A human life summed up in a handful of words, a philosophy to live and die by captured in a phrase, a mystery unsolved for centuries – any tombstones might provide such a prize.

Sometimes I wondered how I should react if, one day, peering at a fading inscription, I deciphered the name, 'Donald Sinden'. Where would such a discovery lead me? Finding a long-lost namesake might lead me to learn more about my own family but any of those gravestones, regardless of the name they bore, could carry a message for me. Here lay the details of hatchings, matchings and dispatchings.

If you will permit a small digression, I came across a splendid example of the latter in the burial register from the parish of Salehurst, Sussex, which read as follows:

10.3.1808

William Sinden aged 39. Blown into five parts.
His head. Leg and thigh. Body and one leg and thigh.
Arm and Arm. From the sudden explosion at Brede
Gunpowder Mills, 7th March.

The births and weddings were fascinating but what
interesting deaths our ancestors met! Life could be cut
short by sky rockets, damp beds, bananas, poisoned bread
and butter, thin shoes and 'derty grass'. Surrounded by
such dangers, our forefathers did well to survive, let alone
pass on the advice preserved on these tablets of stone.

Let us open the account with a timely warning from St
Mary's Church, Bury St Edmunds:

Sarah ye wife of Ed Warton
Dyed ye 7 of Nov 1698 Aged 69
Good people all as you pass by
Looke round, as how corpses do lye
For as you are some time were we
And as we are so must you be

Our interest in the causes of death are far more prosaic
now that they are informed by a veneer of medical
knowledge. In the past the process had a truly morbid
fascination:

To the memory of Ric. Richards
Who by gangrene lost first
A toe afterwards a leg
And lastly his life
On 7th day of Aprill 1656
A cruel death to make three
meals of one
To taste and taste till

all was gone
But know thou Tyrant
When the trumpe shall call
He'll find his feet
& stand when thou shall fall.

Legs had a part to play in this demise as well:

Poor Martha Snell, her's gone away,
Her would if her could, but her couldn't stay,
Her had two bad legs and a baddish cough,
But her legs it was that carried her off.

Here it was one cough too many:

Here lie I bereft of breath
Because a cough
Carried me off;
Then a coffin
They carried me off in.

Whereas this deceased son of Leyland in Lancashire paid
the price of failing to follow natural instincts:

Let the wind go free
Whe'er thou be
For 'twas the wind
That killed me.

Even taking a rest could be fatal if you sat in the wrong
place:

My death did come to pass
Thro' sitting on the derty grass;
Here I lie where I fell,
If you seek my soul go to Hell.

Other causes of death were a source of constant interest, particularly the violent or accidental ones. Some were recorded laconically, like one in Boot Hill Cemetery, Dodge City:

Played five aces
Now playing the harp.

or this from the aptly named Tombstone, Arizona:

Here lies
Lester Moore
Four slugs from a 44
no Les
no more

and this from Frodsham, Cheshire:

Here lies
Jonathan Fry
Killed by a sky-
Rocket in my eye-
Socket.

The force of gravity was responsible for another untimely departure in Eastwell, Kent:

Fear God
Keep the Commandment
And
Don't attempt to climb a tree,
For that's what caused the death of me.

Even the righteous could be struck down without warning, as this inscription from Bury St Edmunds shows:

Here lies interred the body of
Mary Haselton
A young maiden of this town
Born of Roman Catholic parents
And virtuously brought up
Who being in the act of prayer
Repeating her verses
Was instantaneously killed by a flash
of lightning Aug 16 1785
Age 9 years

Recently arrived products of the Industrial Revolution were a menace too:

In crossing o'er the fatal bridge
John Morgan he was slain.
But it was not by mortal hand
But by a railway train.

'Mortal hands' had their part to play all too often, even in Long Buckby, Northamptonshire:

She was a lady of spiritual and cultivated mind and her death was instantaneous, arising from fright occasioned by a violent attack made upon her house door by three or four men in a state of intoxication with a view to disturb the peaceful inmates in the dead of night.

From Plainsfield, Vermont, comes this sad tale of a watery grave:

This blooming youth in health most fair
To his uncle's mill-pond did repair
Undressed himself and so plunged in
But never did come out again.

Another American graveyard, at Winslow in the seaboard state of Maine, records (somewhat ambivalently) another death by drowning:

Here lies the body of John Mound
Lost at sea and never found.

While the Yorkshire fishing port, Whitby, includes in its churchyard a tombstone with the inscription:

Sudden and unexpected was the end,
of our esteemed and beloved friend.
He gave all his friends a sudden shock,
By one day falling into Sunderland Dock.

Death stalked the most tranquil rural pastimes:

To all my friends I bid adieu:
A more sudden death you never knew:
As I was leading the old mare to drink,
She kicked and killed me quicker'n a wink.

Some people were not safe in their own bathrooms:

Here lie the bones of Richard Lawton
Whose death, alas! was strangely brought on.
Trying his corns one day to mow off,
His razor slipped and cut his toe off,
His toe, or, rather what it grew to,

An inflammation quickly flew to.
Which took, alas! to mortifying,
And was the cause of Richard's dying.

Some ignored old proverbs to their cost:

Beneath this stone, this lump of clay,
Lies Uncle Peter Daniels,
Who too early in the month of May
Took off his winter flannels.

Those who had, perhaps, too great an enthusiasm for
life were fondly remembered in many tributes, some
touching, others cautionary:

Gentle Reader, Gentle Reader,
Look on the spot where I do lie,
I was always a very good feeder
But now the worms do feed on I.

This message from the grave comes from a former son
of Wolverhampton:

Here lie the bones
Of Joseph Jones
Who ate while he was able;
But once o'er fed
He dropt down dead,
And fell beneath the table.
When from the tomb
To meet his doom
He rises amidst sinners:
Since he must dwell
In heav'n or hell
Take him – which gives best dinners.

Ironically eating fruit could be hazardous, as in this instance:

> This disease you ne'er heard tell on,
> I died of eating too much melon;
> Be careful, then, all you that feed, I
> Suffered because I was too greedy.

and in this:

> Here lies the body of our Anna
> Done to death by a banana.
> It wasn't the fruit that laid her low
> But the skin of the thing that made her go.

The imagery of fruit adds poignancy to this demise brought about by an apparently innocent beverage:

> Here lies, cut down like unripe fruit,
> The wife of Deacon Amos Shute.
> She died of drinking too much coffee,
> Anno Dominy eighteen forty.

Where drinking is concerned the majority of epitaphs concentrate on the ravages of more potent brews:

> Weep not for me, the warmest tear that's shed
> Falls unavailing o'er the unconscious dead;
> Take the advice the friendly lines would give,
> Live not to drink, but only drink to live.

Nor were members of the cloth immune:

Here lies John Tyrwitt
A learned divine,
He died in a fit
Through drinking port wine.

In days gone by treatments were often as fatal as ailments:

Here lies the body of Mary Ann Lowder
She burst while drinking a seidlitz powder,
Called from this world to her heavenly rest,
She should have waited till it effervesced.

Well known cures could not always be relied on:

Here lie I with my three daughters
Who died drinking Cheltenham waters.
If we had stuck to Epsom Salt,
We should not sleep in this cold vault.

Sometimes the prescription was at fault:

Donald Robertson.
He was a peaceable quiet man and to all appearance
a sincere Christian.
His death was very much regretted –
which was caused by the stupidity
of Lawrence Tuloch of Clotherton
who sold him nitre instead of Epsom Salts by
which he was killed in the space of three hours
after taking a dose of it.

Sometimes it was not even a formal prescription:

———

William Newberry
Who was hostler to an inn
and died in 1695
in consequence of having taken
Improper medicine given him by
a fellow servant.

And sometimes the deceased (mistakenly?) avoided treatment altogether:

Here lies one who for medicine would not give
A little gold: and so his life he lost:
I fancy that he'd wish again to live
Did he but know how much his funeral cost.

So much for the various causes of death. Many tombstones record salient features of the lives of those who lied buried beneath. These can be pretty varied too. Physical features were popular:

Mouths

Here lies a man, as God shall me save,
Whose mouth was wide, as is his grave;
Reader tred lightly o'er his sod,
For, if he gapes, you're gone, by G—d.

Feet

Here lies a man of good repute
Who wore a No 16 boot.
'Tis not recorded how he died,
But sure it is, that open wide,
The gates of Heaven must have been
To let such monstrous feet within.

And girth

> In memory of
> Mrs Alpha White
> Weight 309 lbs
> Open wide ye heavenly gates
> That lead to the heavenly shore;
> Our father suffered in passing through
> And mother weighs much more.

For reasons that we can only guess at women who died
with their maidenly virtues intact were a regular cause of
comment. In Hughley in Shropshire you can read:

> Here lieth the body of Martha Dias
> Always busy and not very pious;
> Who lived the age of three score and ten
> And gave to worms what she refused to men.

From St Pancras, London, comes:

> Here lies (the Lord have mercy on her!)
> One of Her Majesty's maids of honour:
> She was young, slender and pretty;
> She died a maid – the more the pity.

A Welsh churchyard recounts:

> Here lies
> Poor Charlotte
> Who died no harlot
> But in her Virginity
> Of the age Nineteen
> In this vicinity
> Rare to be found or seen.

And this daughter of Warrington was spared by nature herself:

Margaret Robinson, 1816
This maid no elegance of form possessed;
No earthly love defil'd her sacred breast;
Hence free she liv'd from the deceiver man;
Heaven meant it as a blessing; she was plain.

In contrast was the dreadful fate awaiting those who succumbed to passion as this chilling example from St Mary's, Bury St Edmunds, warns:

Reader
Pause at this humble stone
It records the fall of unguarded youth.
By the allurement of vice
And the treacherous snares
of seduction.
Sarah Lloyd
on the 23 of April 1800
in the 22 year of her age
Suffered a just but ignominious death
for admitting her abandoned seducer
into the dwelling house of her mistress
In the night of 3 Oct 1799
And becoming the instrument
In his hands of the crimes
Of robbery and house burning
These were her last words
May my example be a
Warning to thousands

It's natural to find the majority of tombstones erected by

husbands, wives and close relatives. What does come as a surprise is the candour with which some are willing to expose their private past to complete strangers centuries later:

> The children of Israel wanted bread,
> And the Lord he sent them manna,
> Old clerk Wallace wanted a wife,
> And the devil sent him Anna.

Death did not have much of sting for a bereaved Dorset husband:

> Who far beneath this tomb doth rest,
> Has joined the army of the blest.
> The Lord has Ta'en her to the Sky,
> The saints rejoice – and so do I.

Death seemed to leave this Gloucestershire husband completely indifferent to his loss:

> My wife is dead, and here she lies
> Nobody laughs, nobody cries;
> Where she has gone, or how she fares,
> Nobody knows, and nobody cares.

This wife's death brought peace all round:

> Here lies, thank God, a woman who
> Quarrelled & stormed her whole life through;
> Tread gentle o'er her mouldering form,
> Or else you'll cause another storm.

By some accounts deceased wives were not much worse off in the grave than in marriage:

Grieve not for me, my husband dear,
I am not dead but sleepest here,
With patience wait, prepare to die,
And in a short time you'll come to I.

Added by husband some years later;

I am not grieved my dearest life;
Sleep on, I have another wife;
Therefore I cannot come to thee,
For I must go and live with she.

Potterne in Wiltshire, yielded a headstone with a name
that caught my eye, for quite the wrong reason I'm sure:

Here lieth
Mary – the wife of John Ford
We hope her soul is gone to the Lord
But if for Hell she has changed this life
She had better be there than be John Ford's wife.

Then there were those with a more pragmatic approach:

Sacred to the memory of
Jared Bates
who died Aug. the 6th 1800.
His widow, aged 24, lives as 7 Elm Street,
has every qualification for a good wife, and
yearns to be comforted.

That good lady lived in Lincoln, Maine. Thirty years
earlier Charles Ward had been buried in Lowestoft,
buried and soon forgotten:

In memory of
Charles Ward

who died May 1770
aged 63 years.
A dutiful son
A loving brother and
An affectionate husband.
N.B. This stone was not erected by Susan his wife. She erected a stone to John Salter her second husband forgetting the affection of Charles Ward, her first husband.

A good many epitaph writers found inspiration in people's names. A headstone in Dunoon presented an insurmountable challenge:

Here lies the remains of Thomas Woodhen
The most amiable of husbands and excellent of men.
His real name was Woodcock
but it wouldn't come in rhyme.

One in Falkirk proved to be more satisfactory:

Here under this sod and under these trees
Is buried the body of Solomon Pease.
But here in his hole lies only his pod
His soul is shelled out and gone up to God.

And Bath Abbey offers this example:

Here lies Ann Mann;
She lived an old maid and
She died an Old Mann.

On occasions the epitaph writer could draw on the deceased's occupation to supply an appropriate theme.

One of my favourites is the inscription on the tombstone
of the actor Douglas Quayle, a marvellous character actor
of the old school, with whom I worked during the war.
This reads simply:

> Douglas Quayle
> Actor
> Resting

which must be every actor's dream of an epitaph.

Another good example comes from Bolsover, Derbyshire:

> Here lies in a horizontal position the outside case
> of Thomas Hinde clock and watch maker.
> Who departed this life wound up
> in hope of being taken in hand
> by his Maker and being repaired and
> set a-going in the world to come.
> On the 15th of August 1836
> in the nineteenth year of his life.

Here is another from Philadelphia:

> The body of
> Benjamin Franklin
> Printer
> (Like the cover of an old book,
> its contents torn out
> And stript
> of its lettering and gilding)
> Lies here, food for worms
> But the work itself
> shall not be lost

For it will, as he believed
appear once more
In a new
and more elegant edition
Revised and corrected
By
The Author.

In Norwich a domestic servant sent this message from the grave:

Here lies a poor woman who always was tired.
She lived in a house where help wasn't hired:
Her last words on earth were: 'Dear friends I am going
To where there's no cooking, or washing, or sewing,
For everything there is exact to my wishes,
For where they'd don't eat there's no washing of dishes.
I'll be where loud anthems will always be ringing,
But having no voice I'll be quit of the singing.
Don't mourn for me now, don't mourn for me never,
I'm going to do nothing for ever and ever.'

In one case a bereaved husband could at least turn his loss to some advantage:

Here lies Jane Smith, wife of Thomas Smith, marble cutter. This monument was erected by her husband as a tribute to her memory and a specimen of his work. Monuments of the same style 350 dollars.

The most engaging inscriptions are often those which unintentionally convey quite the wrong message, like this from Edinburgh:

Erected to the memory of
John McFarlane

Drown'd in the Water of Leith
By a few affectionate friends.

or this from Saratoga, New York:

Erected to the memory of
John Philips
accidentally shot as a mark
of affection by his brother.

or this from Woolwich:

Sacred to the memory of
Major James Brush
who was killed by the
accidental discharge of
a pistol by his orderly
14th April 1831
well done
good and faithful servant.

and this splendid tribute to the many-wived Mormon leader at his home at Whitingham, Vermont:

Brigham Young
Born on this spot
1801
A man of great courage
and superb equipment.

The Marquis of Anglesey lost a leg at the battle of Waterloo, where it was buried with this epitaph composed in its memory:

Here rests – and let no saucy knave
Presume to sneer and laugh,

To learn that mouldering in the grave
Is laid – a British calf.

And now in England, just as gay
As in the battle brave,
He goes to rout, review and play,
With one foot in the grave.

In Scotland the writer of this epitaph adopted an open-minded approach to the life hereafter:

Here lie I Martin Elginbrodde,
Hae mercy on my soul Lord God
As I wad so were I lord God
And ye were Martin Elginbrodde.

Not all epitaphs are composed to be used as memorials to the dead. A lot of people have had a lot of fun making them up for themselves as well as others.

The Earl of Rochester, Restoration poet, courtier and notorious rake, composed this for Charles II:

Here lies our sovereign Lord the King,
Whose word no man relies on,
Who never said a foolish thing
Nor ever did a wise one.

Robert Benchley wrote this for a promiscuous actress:

At last she sleeps alone.

Johnny Carson, the chat show host, thought this appropriate for his own headstone:

I'll be right back.

W C Fields chose:

On the whole I'd rather be in Philadelphia.

Clark Gable liked:

Back to the silents.

Frederic March settled on:

This is my lot.

As a final offering, here are a selection of last words that also never were, attributed to dozens of God's dumb creatures:

The Bird of Paradise – 'I want to go home.'
The Cat – 'Quick a recount! That was surely only eight.'
The Chameleon – 'Why am I turning red?'
The Crocodile – 'This is no time for tears.'
The Dodo – 'Oh my children! My poor dead children.'
The Dog – 'Just lay me by those bones.'
The Fatted Calf – 'I hear the young master has returned.'
The Lemming – 'We can't all be wrong.'
The Ostrich – 'Just bury me in the sand.'
The Phoenix – 'Cremation, please.'
The Python – 'We must all shuffle off these mortal coils.'
The Turkey – 'If I don't see you before then, have a Happy Christmas!'

To which I can only add:

THE END